UNDERSTANDING
CONTEMPORARY AMERICAN SCIENCE FICTION

Understanding Contemporary American Literature
Matthew J. Bruccoli, Series Editor

Volumes on

Edward Albee • Sherman Alexie • Nicholson Baker • John Barth
Donald Barthelme • The Beats • The Black Mountain Poets • Robert Bly
Raymond Carver • Fred Chappell • Chicano Literature
Contemporary American Drama
Contemporary American Horror Fiction
Contemporary American Literary Theory
Contemporary American Science Fiction, 1926–1970
Contemporary American Science Fiction, 1970–2000
Contemporary Chicana Literature
Robert Coover • James Dickey • E. L. Doctorow • John Gardner
George Garrett • John Hawkes • Joseph Heller • Lillian Hellman
John Irving • Randall Jarrell • Charles Johnson • Adrienne Kennedy
William Kennedy • Jack Kerouac • Ursula K. Le Guin • Denise Levertov
Bernard Malamud • Bobbie Ann Mason • Jill McCorkle
Carson McCullers • W. S. Merwin • Arthur Miller
Toni Morrison's Fiction • Vladimir Nabokov • Gloria Naylor
Joyce Carol Oates • Tim O'Brien • Flannery O'Connor • Cynthia Ozick
Walker Percy • Katherine Anne Porter • Richard Powers
Reynolds Price • Annie Proulx • Thomas Pynchon
Theodore Roethke • Philip Roth • May Sarton • Hubert Selby, Jr.
Mary Lee Settle • Neil Simon • Isaac Bashevis Singer
Jane Smiley • Gary Snyder • William Stafford • Robert Stone
Anne Tyler • Kurt Vonnegut • David Foster Wallace
Robert Penn Warren • James Welch • Eudora Welty
Tennessee Williams • August Wilson

UNDERSTANDING
CONTEMPORARY AMERICAN SCIENCE FICTION

The Age of Maturity,
1970–2000

Darren Harris-Fain

University of South Carolina Press

© 2005 University of South Carolina

Published in Columbia, South Carolina,
by the University of South Carolina Press

Manufactured in the United States of America

09 08 07 06 05   5 4 3 2 1

Library of Congress Cataloging-in-Publication Data

Harris-Fain, Darren.
  Understanding contemporary American science fiction : the age of
maturity, 1970–2000 / Darren Harris-Fain.
       p. cm. — (Understanding contemporary American literature)
    Includes bibliographical references and index.
    ISBN 1-57003-585-7 (alk. paper)
    1. Science fiction, American—History and criticism.   2. American
fiction—20th century—History and criticism.   I. Title. II. Series.
    PS374.S35H37 2005
    813'.0876208054—dc22

                                                    2005003207

In memory of
Thomas D. Clareson

Contents

Series Editor's Preface

The volumes of *Understanding Contemporary American Literature* have been planned as guides or companions for students as well as good nonacademic readers. The editor and publisher perceive a need for these volumes because much of the influential contemporary literature makes special demands. Uninitiated readers encounter difficulty in approaching works that depart from the traditional forms and techniques of prose and poetry. Literature relies on conventions, but the conventions keep evolving; new writers form their own conventions—which in time may become familiar. Put simply, *UCAL* provides instruction in how to read certain contemporary writers—identifying and explicating their material, themes, use of language, point of view, structures, symbolism, and responses to experience.

The word *understanding* in the titles was deliberately chosen. Many willing readers lack an adequate understanding of how contemporary literature works; that is, what the author is attempting to express and the means by which it is conveyed. Although the criticism and analysis in the series have been aimed at a level of general accessibility, these introductory volumes are meant to be applied in conjunction with the works they cover. They do not provide a substitute for the works and authors they introduce, but rather prepare the reader for more profitable literary experiences.

M. J. B.

Acknowledgments

I would like to thank Shawnee State University for granting me a sabbatical for the spring 2004 quarter, which allowed me to complete work on this volume. I am also grateful to the staff of Shawnee's Clark Memorial Library for their assistance in obtaining needed materials. In addition, students in the science fiction classes I taught at Shawnee, especially those in my junior honors seminar on contemporary American science fiction in winter 2004—Derrick Gray, Justin Isaac, Sarah Tingler, Sarah Walke, and Jené Wright—provided many insights.

For their encouragement, I am particularly grateful to my department chair, Timothy E. Scheurer, and my family, especially my wife, Julie. Finally, for their mentorship in science fiction scholarship, I owe a great debt to Donald M. Hassler, my graduate adviser at Kent State University, and the late Thomas D. Clareson, to whose memory this book is dedicated.

CHAPTER 1

Introduction
Where Others Have Gone Before

In the late 1980s, British science fiction writer John Brunner was invited to speak about science fiction at London's Imperial College; members of the college's Science Fiction Society were especially interested in talking about the new movement labeled cyberpunk. In preparation, Brunner read *Mirrorshades: The Cyberpunk Anthology* (1986), edited by Bruce Sterling. "What really surprised me," he said in a 1995 interview, "was how exact a line of descent I could frame for every one of the stories."[1] Even in a type of science fiction that many contemporary readers and critics hailed (or hated) for its novelty, the influence of earlier science fiction was evident to experienced readers, confirming Donald A. Wollheim's often-cited claim from *The Universe Makers: Science Fiction Today* (1971) that "science fiction builds upon science fiction."[2] Despite the current state of the field—in which many readers of science fiction lack a sense of the field's history, instead consuming the latest product as packaged in series or marketed under brand-name authors—to understand contemporary American science fiction fully, one must realize that, in all its variety, it is the result of decades of science fiction before it.[3]

Since almost all historical or critical studies of science fiction contain the obligatory discussion of definitions and theories of the genre, and since this book is intended for those interested in learning more about the subject, it would not be inappropriate to continue the tradition, albeit briefly. Perhaps the best way to begin such a discussion is to apply what Donald M. Hassler says of Gary Westfahl's analysis in *Cosmic Engineers: A Study of Hard Science Fiction* (1996) to science fiction in general. Westfahl, according to Hassler, "rightly points out that since subgenres are continually evolving and changing (like everything else), the most that can be hoped for are better 'descriptions'—accumulative descriptions."[4] Such a task is complicated by the fact that works that could be considered science fiction were published long before the term "science fiction" came into general use.

Stories and novels that anticipate what editor Hugo Gernsback first called "science fiction" in 1929 appeared in American literature during the nineteenth century in the work of writers such as Edgar Allan Poe, Ambrose Bierce, and Samuel Langhorne Clemens (Mark Twain).[5] Their tales of fantastic voyages in space and time, of invisibility, and of other science fiction tropes in turn were preceded by centuries of related works in European folklore and literature. In addition to disagreement over "definitive" definitions of science fiction, historians and critics debate whether such older works should in fact be labeled science fiction. On the one hand, writers such as L. Sprague de Camp and Catherine Crook de Camp in the revised edition of *The Science Fiction Handbook* (1975) and Lester del Rey in *The World of Science Fiction, 1926–1976: The History of a Subculture* (1979) claim an ancestry for science fiction that stretches back to ancient literatures; on the other hand, writers such as Kingsley Amis in *New Maps of Hell: A Survey of Science Fiction* (1960) and Brian W. Aldiss and David Wingrove in *Trillion Year Spree: The History of Science Fiction* (1986) tend to dismiss such claims, asserting that science fiction is a much more recent phenomenon, the flourishing of which can be attributed to modern scientific and technological events such as the industrial revolution and the theory of evolution.[6]

But what is it, exactly, that distinguishes science fiction from other types of writing? Many people unfamiliar with the genre often suppose that science fiction involves stories set in the future, and indeed, this is true of most SF.[7] However, this fails to delimit the genre adequately, as many stories that most readers would identify as SF are set in the present—H. G. Wells's novel *The War of the Worlds* (1898), with its depiction of a Martian invasion of late Victorian England, is an excellent example— or even the past, as in time-travel stories or alternate histories. The example of Wells relates to another set of presuppositions regarding science fiction, that it includes aliens and/or spaceships, and again this is true of much SF. But this too fails to capture the full potential of the genre, since much science fiction lacks these common tropes.

Then what about the term itself, "science fiction"? Is it fiction with substantial scientific content? Well, yes and no. For one thing, it is possible for a work of fiction to focus extensively on science but not be what one would think of as science fiction. For instance, both Sinclair Lewis's *Arrowsmith* (1925) and Richard Powers's *Galatea 2.2* (1995) are centered on science and scientists, but neither is exactly science fictional, although both inhabit the borders between science fiction and realistic fiction, especially the latter (discussed in chapter 5).

It is here that we are able to make our first real distinction. In noting that science fiction is not realistic, in the sense that it includes elements that neither exist in the present nor have existed in the known past, science fiction is not an example of realism (either contemporary or historical) but of the fantastic. Specifically, the "fantastic" refers to a branch of narrative that includes elements that in one way or another depart from the world as we know it. Many people incorrectly identify this counterpart to mimetic fiction as fantasy, and moreover incorrectly classify science fiction as a subgenre of fantasy. It is more accurate, however, to speak of both fantasy and science fiction as subgenres of the fantastic. Both are nonrealistic forms of fiction, but apart from their shared fantastic natures, the two are significantly different. Fantasy literature includes elements that never have existed in the world as we know it and, because of the laws of nature, never can. Thus, for example, J. R. R. Tolkien's *Lord of the Rings* (1954–55) and J. K. Rowling's Harry Potter series (1997–), with their use of magical powers and supernatural creatures, would clearly be fantasy. By contrast, science fiction includes elements that do not exist and have not existed in the past, but that plausibly could exist in the future (or even, in cases such as alien-contact or disaster stories, in the present) or could have existed in the past if the direction of history had been altered. For example, in Rowling's *Harry Potter and the Chamber of Secrets* (1998), a car flies by magic; a science fiction story might also include a flying car, but it would be presented as technologically plausible as opposed to magical. Similarly, an alternate-history story might present a world in which Nazi Germany won World War II. Obviously this is fantastic rather than realistic, but it would be considered science fiction rather than fantasy if the author could provide or at least suggest a plausible explanation for the historical difference and then convincingly extrapolate the consequences.

This idea that science fiction is both plausible and nonrealistic is central to what is perhaps the best-known theoretical definition of the subgenre, proposed by critic Darko Suvin in his *Metamorphoses of Science Fiction: On the Poetics and History of a Literary Genre* (1979). He argued that SF is a literature of "cognitive estrangement," meaning that it is both nonrealistic—that is, it presents readers with settings and situations that are alien to them, from which they are estranged—as well as understandable; in other words, the estrangement can be explained, for the most part, in logical or rational terms. The element that introduces this sense of estrangement Suvin terms the "novum," the new thing. Thus, to return to the flying car example, reading about a flying car in the Harry Potter series indeed offers a sense of estrangement, but this novum cannot be rationally or logically explained, whereas in a science fiction setting such an idea could be not only different (estrangement) but also understandable within the context of implied technological developments that may occur in the future (cognitive). Suvin's definition, it should be noted, also allows for such things as SF stories set in the present (for instance, in Wells's *War of the Worlds,* the novum is the Martians and their technology, intruding into late Victorian England) or the past (in an alternate-history novel, the novum would be the different historical turning from which the author extrapolates a divergent historical track).

Such views of the definition of SF typically lead to pronouncements about its nature. What, after all, introduces the types of radical yet recognizable difference that Suvin discusses? Science, of course, is one response—not only the physical sciences, and the technology that derives from them, but also the social sciences. Much SF depicts societies that have been as transformed by social changes as they have by scientific or technological developments. More broadly speaking, some would say that science fiction is a literature of change—radical, evolutionary change. A key facet of dealing with such change, many critics would argue, is the fact that SF writers are able to both posit radical changes in their stories and extrapolate the possibilities that might result.

Given the general nature of science fiction, then, it is understandable that writers of SF bring to their task not only the standard conventions of fiction but also the generic conventions of the science fiction field as well as the ability to employ scientific fact, extrapolation, and imagination. This set of assumptions for the science fiction writer is neatly summed up by an aspiring writer of the far future in Norman Spinrad's *Child of Fortune* (1985):

> What I have learned best is how much there is to learn before I may truly style myself a maestra of the literary art! Scientific knowledge sufficient to accurately describe arcane events and venues, the annals of the art itself, lest I find myself repeating the stories of others innocently unaware, the millennial history of our species in order to sift truth from hyperbole, the inner meanings of words and images.[8]

The nature of science fiction as a genre begs the question, Why would anyone write something like this, and why would people read it? In her introduction to *The Alternate History,* Karen Hellekson says, "Science fiction asks, 'What if the world were somehow different?'"[9] Fantasy asks the same question, but implied in Hellekson's comparison of science fiction in general and alternate history in particular is the notion that this difference can be rationally explained with no violation of cause and effect as we understand them. But it is this very notion of cause and effect that leads to the question. If things change (as we know they do, through historical, sociological, and scientific study), and if such change can be explained, one implication of this is that there are multiple possibilities for the ways things can become and, in alternate history, of they way things could have happened in the past. Extrapolated into the future, this has led writers to explore the manifold ways in which the future might develop (which also helps to explain the abundance of futures to be found in science fiction, including contradictory visions). With alternate history, this extrapolation takes place using historical events, and with science fiction stories set in the present, writers imagine how the intrusion of some possible or at least plausible event might change the world as we now know it.

The imaginative exploration of possible change has value for itself, for both the entertaining stories that can result and the exercise of imagination. But there has often been more to the motives behind SF than this. Science fiction has often been a literature of satire, critique, social commentary, or warning. If one considers a work of proto-SF such as Jonathan Swift's *Gulliver's Travels* (1726), for example, one can easily see how Swift employs the fantastic to comment upon his own world. Similarly, cold war–era films such as *The Day the Earth Stood Still* (1951) and *Invasion of the Body Snatchers* (1956) can easily be interpreted as parables regarding the threat of nuclear war and conformity or the fear of Communist infiltration, respectively. While most SF is less obvious in its critique of social, political, religious, or scientific issues, nonetheless a major impetus behind the genre has been how it allows authors to comment upon contemporary concerns in the guise of a story that on the surface is far removed from the here and now, which helps to explain why some of the most penetrating critiques of their government to come from Soviet writers came in the form of science fiction.

Both the desire to entertain and the desire to comment upon contemporary issues as well as religious or philosophical ideas through the guise of the fantastic are evident in earlier works that anticipate science fiction. For instance, the Renaissance produced tales of fantastic voyages to the moon and utopian works; the former serve for the most part as entertainment, while the latter serve as critiques of existing governments and, in some cases, proposals for better ones. A notable later work in both modes is Swift's *Gulliver's Travels*.

It is in the nineteenth century, however, that most historians of science fiction place the true origins of the form. From late Gothic novels such as Mary Wollstonecraft Shelley's *Frankenstein* (1818, revised 1831), credited by Brian W. Aldiss as being the first science fiction novel, to the technological and scientific explorations of Jules Verne to stories dealing with "future wars" to the scientific romances of H. G. Wells, many of the common concerns of what would eventually be called science fiction are first embodied in the 1800s, for the purpose of either entertaining readers or exploring serious ideas about the nature of humanity, society, science, technology, and God—in some instances for both.

It is at the end of the nineteenth century and the beginning of the twentieth that American science fiction begins to become separated from "literary fiction" and to dominate the field. At the turn of the last century, a variety of factors began to reshape the literary landscape in the English-speaking world, particularly in the United States. Toward the end of the nineteenth century, popular magazines catering to the tastes of newly literate masses proliferated. In these publications, which around the turn of the century evolved into inexpensive magazines printed on pulp paper, science fiction as it developed in the United States began to take definite shape. Edgar Rice Burroughs, for instance, published his first novel, *A Princess of Mars* (1917), in *All-Story Magazine* in 1912 as "Under the Moons of Mars." Essentially an action-adventure story with an alien setting and characters, it defined, according to Aldiss, one pole of science fiction.[10]

Contrasted with this, says Aldiss, is another type of American science fiction that emerged early in the twentieth century, focusing on technology. The primary advocate of this kind of science fiction was Gernsback, who with *Amazing Stories* in 1926 founded the first magazine devoted entirely to science fiction, or, as he called it at the time, "scientifiction." The early issues of the magazine featured reprints of works by Poe, Verne, and Wells, but Gernsback also sought new material, and soon authors who were publishing their science fiction stories and serialized novels in general-audience magazines began concentrating on the new science fiction magazine and its imitators as an easier market, and readers soon discovered them as a concentrated source for stories they enjoyed. As an editor, Gernsback sought to publish stories in which technology was prominent; the plots and characterizations thus tended toward the formulaic.[11] Nonetheless, as James Gunn and Gary Westfahl have argued, Gernsback deserves credit for helping to shape and promote science fiction as a genre, despite the later criticisms he has received for his editorial limitations. New magazines, in particular *Astounding Science-Fiction,* appeared in the 1930s, but for the most part American science fiction was driven by action and adventure in exotic settings and/or by gadgetry, whether realistic or farfetched, until the late 1930s, which many fans and critics consider the beginning of the Golden Age of SF.

Many critics link this Golden Age with the assumption of John W. Campbell Jr. to the editorship of *Astounding Science-Fiction* in 1937. To be sure, Campbell's interest in publishing stories that could be read as realistic by an audience centuries in the future led to more carefully detailed stories, but the Golden Age would not have happened were it not for the work of established writers who continued to hone their craft, such as Jack Williamson and Murray Leinster, as well as newer writers, such as Isaac Asimov and Robert A. Heinlein, who knew how to tell good stories that just happened to be SF. In style, characterization, and plotting, their work resembled not that of such prominent contemporary authors as William Faulkner, F. Scott Fitzgerald, or Ernest Hemingway but rather that of an earlier generation of writers, such as Poe, Robert Louis Stevenson, Twain, and Wells. While progressive in many of their ideas, in their writing these science fiction authors were fairly conservative and, in the case of less-successful writers, fairly crude—another trait that led many critics, when they noticed science fiction at all, to dismiss it as unsophisticated if not subliterary.

Though for the most part relegated to pulp magazines and looked down upon by much of the American public, American science fiction during the late 1930s and the 1940s began to mature—as did its readership, which grew from being dominated by adolescent boys and young men interested in science and adventure to a broader audience interested in what had become a recognizable genre. During the 1940s, American SF began to expand its borders, with some writers (most notably Heinlein) placing stories in "slick" magazines such as the *Saturday Evening Post* and writing juvenile SF novels for major trade publishers. In addition, SF books appeared and flourished in the rapidly growing paperback market of the late 1940s and the 1950s as well as through small fan presses.

American SF made even further inroads into mainstream American culture during the 1950s. Popular movies such as *Destination Moon* (1950), *The Thing* (1951), and *The Day the Earth Stood Still* were all based on magazine stories and novels, and original films such as *Forbidden Planet* (1956), based loosely on William Shakespeare's *The Tempest* (c. 1611) and popular understandings of Sigmund Freud, were also successful. Television and paperback books, media that became popular during the 1940s, prominently featured SF, and writers such as Asimov, Heinlein, and especially Ray Bradbury achieved a level of general fame during the decade that was unprecedented for the field. Bradbury was hailed as a visionary by the likes of Christopher Isherwood and C. S. Lewis, and his work began appearing more frequently in such magazines as *Playboy* than in SF magazines. Walter M. Miller Jr.'s novel *A Canticle for Leibowitz* (1960), about a monastic order that attempts to salvage civilization after a series of nuclear wars, also received favorable attention from outside the field as well as within it.

As American SF began appearing more frequently in books, the magazines began to decline in popularity, though not for that reason alone. Newer periodicals such as the *Magazine of Fantasy and Science Fiction* (founded in 1949) and *Galaxy* (founded in 1950) flourished within the field and older ones such as *Astounding Science-Fiction* held on, but the magazines tended to remain in the SF ghetto even as some SF writers began to break out of it. In addition, the pulp magazines that nurtured American SF died during the 1950s, unable to compete with television, comic books, and paperbacks. The magazines that survived did so in other formats, most notably digest-sized periodicals.

Late in the 1950s, American SF also began to attract serious critical attention. Writer-critics such as Damon Knight and James Blish (writing as William Atheling Jr.) subjected contemporary American SF to scrutinizing critiques, while British author Kingsley Amis lauded much American SF in a series of lectures that were published as *New Maps of Hell: A Survey of Science Fiction.*[12] Academe also began to notice SF as a subject of serious study. In 1958, Thomas D. Clareson established a meeting on SF at the annual Modern Language Association convention, and the following year he founded *Extrapolation,* the first academic journal devoted to the genre. Others would follow in later years, notably *Science Fiction Studies* in the United States and *Foundation* in Great Britain.

By the early 1960s, SF was being taught on some American campuses, and other signs of its expansion and wider acceptance became evident. Heinlein's 1961 novel *Stranger in a Strange Land,* like J. R. R. Tolkien's three-volume fantasy *Lord of the Rings* a campus favorite during the decade, was the first American work of SF to reach the *New York Times Book Review* best-seller list, and writers such as Asimov and Bradbury continued to reach audiences beyond SF fandom. Major publishing houses, which had toyed with SF since the 1940s but had not yet invested in it heavily, found the form to be profitable as more and more people read it for pleasure.

While genre categorization was favored by publishers, bookstores, public libraries, and many fans, some writers began to recoil against what they saw as the continued ghettoization of the field. Unlike many of the more established American SF writers, who often were trained in science and technology, several of the younger writers who began to emerge during the late 1950s and early 1960s possessed a more consciously literary bent. Rebelling against the widespread public image of science fiction as stories devoid of literary merit that featured spaceships, ray guns, and bug-eyed monsters (a notion Canadian author Margaret Atwood perpetuated in her remarks about her 2003 novel *Oryx and Crake,* which she labeled "speculative fiction" instead), these writers of SF's "New Wave" drew upon the shift of some authors of the 1950s toward social sciences such as sociology and psychology and upon the literary techniques of modernism and occasionally postmodernism to create what some of them began to label (anticipating Atwood) "speculative fiction," or SF for short. Heinlein, never considered a New Wave writer though he shared with many New Wave writers a preoccupation with sex and breaking taboos, coined the term "speculative fiction" in a symposium, the proceedings of which were published as *Of Worlds Beyond* (1947), edited by Lloyd Arthur Eshbach. Though Heinlein meant by the term a type of SF involving extrapolation from the known producing "a new situation, a new framework for human action,"[13] in the second half of the 1960s, Judith Merril in her book-review column in *Fantasy and Science Fiction* proposed using the term to define SF that retains that extrapolation while de-emphasizing the hard sciences (at the same time keeping the SF acronym). Taking inspiration from a recent school of young talents in French cinema, critics and anthologists called these younger writers and their fiction the New Wave.[14]

The split between the New Wave and everyone else in American SF during the late 1960s was nearly as dramatic as the division at the same time between young protesters and what they called "the establishment," and in fact, the political views of the younger writers, often prominent in their work, reflect many contemporary concerns. New Wave writers accused what became de facto the old wave of being old-fashioned, patriarchal, imperialistic, and obsessed with technology; many of the more established writers thought the New Wave shallow, said that its literary innovations were not innovations at all (which in fact, outside of SF, they were not), and accused it of betraying SF's grand view of humanity's role in the universe. Both assertions were largely exaggerations, of course, and in the next decade both trends would merge into a synthesis of styles and concerns. However, in 1970 the issue was far from settled and would remain a source of contention for the next few years.

Another situation in American SF since 1970 has its roots in the decade before: the fragmentation of SF fandom.[15] At one time it was possible for fans to both read almost every new story in the major magazines and have a wide reading in older SF works. With the expansion of the market, however, and its spread into other media such as television and—especially after the success of SF movies such as *Star Wars* (1977) and *Close Encounters of the Third Kind* (1977)—motion pictures, only a few writers and fans make a serious effort to stay on top of every new development in the field, even if complete knowledge of everything being published has since become impossible. Moreover, reading everything written about SF by fans was almost an impossibility even in the days of mimeograph and hectograph machines; with the addition of SF journals, as well as online journals, fanzines, and discussion groups since cyberspace, a word coined by William Gibson in his SF story "Burning Chrome" (1982), that task is impossible as well. Further, since 1970, American SF, much like popular music and television, has splintered into a variety of subgenres and categories, and while there are many readers with eclectic tastes who sample many different types of works, it is possible to find readers devoted to a single type of SF, such as military SF, cyberpunk, or works centered around the universe created by *Star Trek* and its spinoffs. It is also possible to find self-proclaimed fans of SF who have never read an SF magazine or SF written before they were born. Thus a writer such as Brunner could detect older influences in a type of SF that many readers believed was like nothing else done before.

While the diversification of American SF helps in some ways to assure it an ongoing market by appealing to a broader set of demographics, many writers and critics fear that the SF that sells to its own built-in market will drive out more original or more demanding work. Indeed, it is often discouraging for many authors and SF scholars to see shelves full of competent but not terribly original books while older SF classics and interesting newer works go out of print. The situation is not entirely bleak, however, as some older works have reappeared in handsome paperback editions or even in hardcover. More important for American SF since 1970, there have been several works of considerable merit published, and good work continues to appear. The late science fiction writer Theodore Sturgeon once formulated what has come to be known as Sturgeon's Law. "Ninety percent of science fiction is crap," he supposedly said, "but then, ninety percent of *everything* is crap." If this is true (and critic Gary Westfahl has questioned its validity, arguing that "science fiction, overall, generates a smaller percentage of crap than other fields of literature"), the logical corollary is that 10 percent of everything is not bad or even pretty good, including contemporary SF.[16] Finding that 10 percent, or whatever the percentage may be, among the proliferation of books and magazines that now exists is something of a challenge or a chore, but it can be done. The chapters that follow bring to light a fraction of those works and writers deserving of attention while placing them within the larger context of the directions American SF has taken since 1970.

This book's limited focus on a fraction of noteworthy or representative works written for an adult readership—abundant examples of science fiction written for children and young adults also exist—is a practical necessity, both because of the scope of the UCAL series format and because it is impossible for any one reader at this point in the history of science fiction to have read everything that has been published, even if one is able to weed out the 90 percent or so of crap. One of the key facets of American science fiction since 1970 is not just its diversity but also its remarkable abundance. This book provides a glimpse at this abundance and an overview of the general lay of the land to allow readers to contextualize other works they might read in the future, but comprehensiveness is not the goal here.

In addition to discussions of contemporary American science fiction, along with suggestions for future reading, listed in the bibliography, certain resources in particular deserve recommendation. Michael M. Levy provides a good overview of the period in his chapter in the fourth edition of Neil Barron's *Anatomy of Wonder* (1995), in which Levy and Brian Stableford annotate hundreds of noteworthy titles. Aldiss and Wingrove provide interesting discussions of contemporary American science fiction up to the mid-1980s in *Trillion Year Spree* (1986); other valuable historical resources include Edward James's *Science Fiction in the 20th Century* (1994), Brooks Landon's *Science Fiction after 1900* (1997), and the historical chapters in *The Cambridge Companion to Science*

Fiction (2003), edited by James and Farah Mendlesohn. For more-detailed treatments of developments in American science fiction year by year, one should look at the annually published *Year's Best Science Fiction,* edited by Gardner Dozois, which include not only significant examples of the fiction but also essays on recent developments and Dozois's knowledgeable overviews. Finally, for even more information on current writers, works, and trends, one should consult the *New York Review of Science Fiction* and especially *Locus,* a monthly news magazine devoted to science fiction and fantasy. Of course, in understanding any field of literature, there is no substitute for reading the texts themselves, and readers interested in learning more about the subject should use this book not only as an overview of the topic but also as a source of significant titles to be read.

Finally, the existence—some would say the omnipresence—of science fiction in media other than print deserves mention. A discussion of nonliterary material is beyond the scope of a book that contributes to a series on contemporary American literature, of course, but a greater abundance of science fiction in media such as motion pictures, radio shows, television, comics, and video and computer games exists than in any other genre with the possible exception of fantasy, and this fact has some bearing on the perception of science fiction as a literary medium. As Sturgeon noted, science fiction is the only genre that is judged by its worst examples, and it does not much help matters when science fiction literature is judged through the somewhat distorted lens of science fiction movies, TV shows, and so forth. While there are many notable examples of SF in the media, these tend to be the exception rather than the rule, and even adaptations of exemplary science fiction stories and novels generally fail to capture the full qualities of their sources. James remarks in *Science Fiction in the 20th Century* that one cannot understand science fiction in its entirety without considering both literary and nonliterary forms. This book cannot examine the latter, but this is no deficiency: there is plenty of worthwhile American science fiction published since 1970 to keep readers busy for a long, long time.

CHAPTER 2

After the New Wave, 1970–1976

In 1970, American society was in a state of considerable cultural transformation, if not chaos. Campuses were in upheaval, the government was in the midst of an increasingly unpopular war in Vietnam, and the culture reeled under a steady stream of social changes. Similarly, American science fiction was undergoing substantial change. A long-anticipated event within the field, the first moon landing, in 1969, was virtually overshadowed by tensions within American SF over traditionalism versus the New Wave, which began in the late 1960s. In part, the split paralleled the "generation gap" of the period, which many blamed for differences between young people and their elders. Like many young protesters, for example, several SF writers, including several young writers associated with the New Wave, signed a letter published in both the March 1968 issue of the *Magazine of Fantasy and Science Fiction* and the June 1968 issue of *Galaxy Science Fiction* protesting American involvement in the war in Vietnam; another group of SF writers publicly supported American involvement with a signed ad in both magazines.[1]

The New Wave, which included stories that differed from earlier SF in experimenting with more consciously literary techniques and in favoring subjects such as extreme psychological states and explicit sex, continued to operate in several works in the early 1970s. A number of writers and readers dismissed the New Wave as pretentious and pointed out the that winners of the Nebula Awards, created by the Science Fiction Writers of America (SFWA) in 1965, tended to be very different from recipients of the Hugo Awards, given by fans at the annual World Science Fiction Convention (the Worldcon), arguing that this highlighted the fact that many writers had departed from readers' tastes into self-indulgence. To be sure, the earnestness of many of the New Wave's proponents echoes the self-importance and limited sense of scope to be found in the sententious proclamations of many minor advocates of literary movements such as British romanticism or American modernism. By 1972—when *Again, Dangerous Visions,* the sequel to the 1967 anthology *Dangerous Visions,* which many critics pointed to as the epitome of the New Wave, was published—Harlan Ellison, editor of both volumes, was saying that such labels were irrelevant and what mattered most was the quality of the writing.

While some writers and fans continued to argue about the New Wave until the end of the 1970s—in *The World of Science Fiction, 1926–1976: The History of a Subculture,* for instance, Lester del Rey devotes several pages to castigating the movement—for the most part the controversy died down as the decade wore on. It seemed as if what did matter most in the field was good writing. Indeed, definitions of what constituted good writing expanded as SF fandom, formerly a fairly tight-knit body despite differences in tastes and personalities, began to fragment into related but often separate groups.

A growing number of readers and fans, for example, became devoted to particular writers or television shows. Thus fans of Isaac Asimov's *I, Robot* (1950) or his Foundation trilogy (1951–53),[2] Robert A. Heinlein's *Stranger in a Strange Land,* or Frank Herbert's *Dune* (1965) became devoted readers of Asimov,

Heinlein, or Herbert. (By the 1980s, all three writers were enjoying sales and even advances in the millions of dollars, an unprecedented achievement for a field in which they once earned pennies a word or even less.) Similarly, fans of the television show *Star Trek* (1966–69), which ended after three seasons due to poor ratings but achieved cult status shortly afterward, could buy at first prose adaptations of *Star Trek* episodes, then new novel-length adventures, such as James Blish's *Spock Must Die!* (1970).[3] In the following years, many writers of SF, along with several fantasy and horror authors, were read by people who would never label themselves fans of these genres in their entirety. Piers Anthony, Terry Brooks, Stephen R. Donaldson, Robert Jordan, and Stephen King grew in popularity in part because of this trend.

Another segment of the American SF market in the 1970s was composed of readers who considered themselves devotees of SF and/or fantasy in general. What was new was that many of these readers enjoyed particular types of fantastic fiction instead of trying to be conversant with an entire genre. Thus the 1960s and 1970s witnessed the beginning of an enthusiasm for J. R. R. Tolkien's wildly popular *Lord of the Rings* that has lasted into the twenty-first century; Peter Jackson's acclaimed cinematic adaptation of the novel (2001–3), also done in three installments, has only added to this popularity. Imitators followed in series after series, and publishers revived older fantasy works with similar themes and styles. This renaissance of fantasy literature, especially fantasy literature of a certain epic stripe, is significant for an understanding of contemporary American SF because it greatly influenced the field: publishers and bookstores linked SF and fantasy more closely than they had ever been connected in the history of American popular culture, and SF writers increasingly crossed over to fantasy or included fantastic elements in their SF.

Nonetheless, for anyone looking for interesting SF between 1970 and 1977, there was plenty to be found. Some of it was influenced by the New Wave aesthetic, some was more traditional, and some combined elements of the two styles. The result was the beginning of a reshaping of American SF in favor of an abundant diversity of theme, style, and quality—a reshaping that has persisted into the twenty-first century.

Although two major awards given in American science fiction, the Hugo and the Nebula, are granted by two very different groups, attendees of the annual Worldcon and members of the SFWA (since 1992, the Science Fiction and Fantasy Writers of America), both selected the same three works for the three major fiction categories for 1970: novel, novella, and short story. These works are surprisingly different from one another. Theodore Sturgeon's short story "Slow Sculpture" includes a scientific element but otherwise reads like a realistic story set in contemporary times; Fritz Leiber's novella *Ill Met in Lankhmar* is closer to sword-and-sorcery fantasy than science fiction; and Larry Niven's novel *Ringworld* is set primarily in outer space centuries in the future and thus comes closest to what most people think of when they think of science fiction.

Sturgeon's "Slow Sculpture," seemingly set in the present, involves an isolated genius who cures a woman he encounters of cancer but is reluctant to share his discovery with a world that places profit over usefulness. He is also reluctant to become involved with the woman, who nonetheless is effective in turning his life in a new direction. The story's title, which refers to the man's bonsai tree, also symbolizes a theme consistent with much of Sturgeon's work: how people can change through human relationships. "Slow Sculpture" is a well-crafted story, worthy of publication in any literary periodical in the country, yet its strong scientific element as well as the author's established reputation as a science fiction writer undoubtedly led Sturgeon to publish it in *Galaxy* rather than the *New Yorker.*

In contrast, Niven's *Ringworld* is much closer to conventional science fiction. The viewpoint character, Louis Wu, is a two-hundred-year-old man who, thanks to "boosterspice," has the body of a man a tenth his age. He is recruited by Nessus, an unusual two-headed alien known as a Puppeteer, to investigate a strange artifact light-years away in exchange for a new technology that will greatly expedite interstellar travel. The expedition also includes Louis's young girlfriend, Teela Brown, who is thought to possess incredible good luck (later revealed as the result of a centuries-long breeding experiment), as well as Speaker-to-Animals, a kzin. The kzinti are large aliens who have bodies like humans yet feline features. They are also humanity's former enemies.

In fact, *Ringworld* is part of a larger tapestry on which Niven and, later, his collaborators have embroidered a sprawling tale of humanity's future and its relationships with other sentient races. Known collectively as Tales of Known Space, this tapestry falls within a category of science fiction called "future history." Over a series of works, an author of future history documents a projected timeline of human history in future centuries or even millennia, typically with specific dates and often with recurring characters or sets of characters. Thus *Ringworld,* with its humans, Puppeteers, and kzinti, and with suggestions of yet other alien races, is part of a larger story of these races' histories and relationships that began with Niven's 1964 story "The Coldest Place" and continued into the twenty-first century, a story that spans from the near future to the thirtieth century.

In addition to being an example of future history, Niven's Tales of Known Space also exemplify another recent trend in American science fiction, the concept of the "shared world." This term designates two types of writing enterprises: sets of stories by various hands occurring in the same fictional universe and coordinated by a creator who invented this universe for just such an enterprise, such as George R. R. Martin's Wild Cards anthologies, begun in 1987, about superheroes in an alternate universe, or expansions by various hands of a fictional universe created by an author who has already developed this universe in his or her own work and who sanctions and oversees such expansions by other writers. Niven's Tales of Known Space fits the latter category, as books that relate the history of the Man-Kzin Wars comprising part of the larger narrative of the sequence are written by other authors in the framework of Niven's future history.

Niven's *Ringworld* is also an example of yet another trend in science fiction that has always existed in the field but received its current label in recent decades: hard SF. According to Allen Steele in his often-quoted essay "Hard Again," published in the June 1992 issue of the *New York Review of Science Fiction,* hard SF "is the form of imaginative literature that uses either established or carefully extrapolated science as its backbone." One might suppose that all science fiction adhered to this dictum, but in fact much science fiction is based neither on existing science nor on carefully extrapolated scientific advancements but rather on what might be called pseudoscientific notions such as extrasensory perception or time travel. Hard SF, in contrast, is more closely related to the so-called hard sciences, such as chemistry and physics. Moreover, the term "hard SF" emerged in juxtaposition and contrast to New Wave science fiction, since the latter tended to draw more heavily on the so-called soft sciences, or social sciences, such as psychology and sociology, than on the more traditional science of much earlier science fiction.

The major "hard" scientific element of Niven's *Ringworld* is the object named in the title, the object that Nessus and the rest of the expedition seek to investigate. The Ringworld is a modified Dyson sphere, an object theorized by physicist Freeman Dyson that would enclose a sun and thus solve two major problems at once, energy limitations and overpopulation. In contrast, the Ringworld is only a ribbon around a star, but it is a ribbon thousands of miles wide and millions of miles in circumference. The characters in *Ringworld* are thus able to explore only a fraction of the enormous enigma, which provides enough material for several adventures.

In fact, the narrative strategy of *Ringworld*, for all the strangeness of the novel's characters and settings, is that of the familiar adventure story, wherein an assorted cast of characters engages in a quest that leads them into a variety of dangers and other interesting situations. In this respect, *Ringworld* resembles the picaresque fantasy novels that began to proliferate in the United States during the 1970s in the wake of the considerable popularity in the 1960s of Tolkien's *The Hobbit* (1938) and *Lord of the Rings*.

Other elements of *Ringworld* are traditional as well, especially Niven's treatment of gender. The viewpoint character, Louis Wu, is no infallible hero, but he nonetheless does heroic things, as does Speaker-to-Animals, who comes from a race of warriors. Both males protect the cowardly Nessus, whose gender is indeterminate, and Teela Brown, who at times is depicted as something close to the conventional damsel in distress.

But while *Ringworld* in many respects is strongly rooted in genre traditions, in other ways the novel challenges or even mocks them. For example, while the sexual acts in the novel are not terribly explicit and Niven quickly cuts to a new scene rather than lingering, there *are* depictions of sex in the novel, in contrast to much earlier science fiction. While *Ringworld* is hardly a New Wave novel, in its treatment of sex—in particular, sex outside of marriage—it is very much a product of its period. Further, at one point in the story, Niven plays with the conventions of heroic science fiction:

> Louis struck an attitude: parade rest. *An inspiration to his crew, the heroic commander stands astride the bridge. The damaged rocket motors may explode at the first touch of thrust; but it must be tried. The kzinti battleships must be stopped before they reach Earth!*
>
> "It'll never work," said Louis Wu.[4]

Thus, while Niven's *Ringworld* is a throwback to much earlier science fiction, the author is aware of some of those conventions and circumvents them through a more contemporary approach to his characters and their story.

Leiber's *Ill Met in Lankhmar* is a throwback of another kind. The novella tells of how Fafhrd and the Gray Mouser—Leiber's most popular characters, whose adventures he had described in a series of stories and novellas since 1937, with the first collections appearing a couple decades later—first met and became a team. No doubt the series' popularity helped this novella win the two major American awards in science fiction despite the fact that it, and the series as a whole, is an example of sword-and-sorcery fantasy, not SF.

The fact that *Ill Met in Lankhmar* won these SF awards also points to another important trend in the field. As discussed in the introduction, both science fiction and fantasy are sub-genres of the fantastic, a subgenre of fiction that, unlike histori-cal or contemporary realism, includes some element that differs from the world as we know it. If realistic or mimetic fiction holds the mirror up to reality, then the fantastic distorts the reflected world in some way. The difference between the two subgenres is that in fantasy, there is at least one impossible ele-ment, at least one thing that never has happened and never could. In contrast, in science fiction there is also something that deviates from the known world, but this element either could have happened in the past (as in alternate history) or could con-ceivably happen now or in the future without violating a plau-sible notion of possibility. Despite this distinction, however, in actual practice the writers and readers of the two subgenres have often been the same people, and in spite of the works' generic differences, their shared fantastic nature has led to their frequent pairing in bookstores and libraries. Thus it is hardly surprising that Leiber, who wrote a lot of science fiction, also spent much of his career writing fantasy. Nor is it surprising that his fellow science fiction writers (those who vote on the Nebula) would be familiar with his fantasy, as would many science fic-tion fans (those who vote on the Hugo). With these facts in mind, it is not difficult to understand why this medieval fantasy involving a large barbarian swordsman and a smaller swords-man who dabbles in magic would be considered for awards devoted to science fiction.

Such decisions have not been entirely without controversy, however, as shown by the dissatisfaction expressed by many in the field when the British author J. K. Rowling received the Hugo in 2002 for *Harry Potter and the Goblet of Fire* (2001). This dissatisfaction stemmed not from her nationality (other

British writers had received the award before, most notably Arthur C. Clarke) nor from the fact that this was a series book or from its juvenile audience, but because the Harry Potter books are clearly fantasy rather than science fiction.

What was different in Leiber's case was not only the long-standing affection his peers and his fans bore him and his stories about Fafhrd and the Gray Mouser but also the period. Medievalized fantasy was experiencing a renaissance, due in large part to the popularity of Tolkien among American readers in the 1960s and 1970s. In the 1960s, Leiber began collecting his older stories about his two heroes and started adding new ones to their number. Thus it is not surprising that this story of his heroes' origins should be better received as a Hugo and Nebula winner than the fourth book of a recent series about a boy wizard, popular though it was.

These three award-winning works by Sturgeon, Niven, and Leiber all came from genre writers, that is to say, authors who identified themselves, primarily through the magazines and publishers to whom they marketed their work, as science fiction and/or fantasy writers. But there are authors who sometimes write science fiction and yet are not considered science fiction writers. They write in a variety of genres, perhaps, or they emerge from the mainstream with a work that is undeniably science fiction, even if the publisher does not market it as such or the author acknowledge it as such. Thus Jack Finney, who in 1955 published *The Body Snatchers,* a story better known in its film incarnations, in 1970 published what many consider one of the finest time-travel stories ever written, *Time and Again.*

In many ways, *Time and Again* looks backward twice. Not only does the story take the protagonist from the 1970s to the 1880s, but how he gets there is reminiscent of an earlier tradition of time-travel stories. Before H. G. Wells's novel *The Time Machine* (1895), which posited scientific theories about the fourth dimension and used a mechanical device to enable the Time Traveler to explore the future, time-travel stories were less concerned with the actual process of temporal travel. For instance, in Mark Twain's *Connecticut Yankee in King Arthur's Court* (1889), the eponymous hero finds himself in medieval England following a blow to the head. Finney, following Wells and numerous others in the intervening decades of such stories, is more scrupulous and, like Wells, throws in some theoretical speculations about the nature of time, but in essence his protagonist, part of a government experiment, simply manages to find himself nearly a century in the past by researching the period, being placed in a setting that duplicated the conditions of late-nineteenth-century New York City, and then wishing himself there.

What is remarkable about Finney's *Time and Again* is not so much the mode of time travel as the results. While the plot is not terribly original, involving political intrigue, some action and adventure, and of course a love story, and while the concept of the character from another time coming to terms with a different time was hardly original by this point in the history of science fiction, the presentation of the setting more than makes up for these facts. Finney presents readers with an 1880s New York that is so vividly realized and depicted that they feel, along with the protagonist, that they truly are there. In fact, *Time and Again* is more a historical novel than a work of science fiction, and in this sense it is comparable to another time-travel novel of the 1970s, Octavia E. Butler's *Kindred* (discussed in chapter 3). Yet part of what makes *Time and Again* so effective is the fact that it is not simply a historical novel in which the characters accept their world as routine. Through the eyes of his time traveler, Finney shows this lost world to be almost as strange and alien as any setting in more conventional works of science fiction.[5]

Also historical in tone is *A Time of Changes* by Robert Silverberg, which received the Nebula Award for best novel of 1971, one of several works of the 1970s in which Silverberg created a new literary identity for himself, seeing himself now more as an artist with goals similar to those articulated by representatives of the New Wave rather than, as he was from the beginning of his career in the 1950s to the late 1960s, a talented and prolific craftsman.

Although readers of *A Time of Changes* eventually learn that the setting is a distant planet in the future, a planet colonized long ago by humans from Earth, initially the first-person narrative, with its description of a society that is somewhat feudal in nature, leads readers in other directions. However, it gradually becomes apparent that this world possesses some technology, specifically "groundcars." Still, the level of technology mentioned in the progress of the story is less advanced than that of the United States in 1971, leaving readers up in the air as to the exact nature and history of this alien world before its actual history is revealed.

Indeed, Silverberg's achievement in building an alien society that is nonetheless recognizably human is perhaps the novel's most significant accomplishment. In this world, self-expression and the sharing of personal feelings are forbidden; even use of the words "I" or "me" is considered vulgar. Some sharing of self is permitted with one's "bondbrother" and "bondsister," and one can bare oneself to the clergy of this world's religion, but by and large the culture supports a sense of self-reliance and even loneliness as the only right and proper path. Added to this is a complex political system and a distinction between the "civilized" inhabitants of the northern continent and the "barbaric" inhabitants of the southern continent. While some critics have faulted the novel for the weakness of its sociology,[6] it nevertheless is a compelling depiction of a world much like our own yet very different.

Most of Silverberg's fiction during the 1970s was concerned not just with future societies but also with psychology. This concern, shared by many contemporary SF writers, led to their work being labeled as dealing with "inner space," as opposed to the stereotypical image of SF as fiction about outer space. In Silverberg's novels and stories, existential issues of alienation and authenticity are combined with imaginative SF stories and settings to produce some of the best work in the field during this period, including *A Time of Changes*.

As can be seen through *A Time of Changes*, much of the value of science fiction lies in the way similarities and differences allow readers to consider their own world from a different perspective. The protagonist of *A Time of Changes*, Kinnall Darival, is very different from readers of the novel, not only in the fact that he has been socialized within an alien culture but also in his noble birth and his forbidden desire for his bondsister. Yet he is also recognizably human in his desires and motivations, as flawed as he often is. In particular, his covert sense of dissatisfaction with the norms of his world renders him susceptible to the temptations offered by the Earthman Schweiz, whose own discontent has led him to a drug this world produces that provides a temporary joining of minds, which he considers a religious experience of a sort that has yet eluded him. Persuaded to try the drug with Schweiz, Kinnall ultimately rebels against his society. Yet Earth as Schweiz describes it hardly offers a more appealing alternative:

> I asked him to tell now about Earth. . . .
>
> "A small planet," he said. "Far away. Choked in its own ancient wastes; the poisons of two thousand years of carelessness and overbreeding stain its skies and its seas and its land. An ugly place."
>
> "In truth, ugly?"
>
> "There are still some attractive districts. Not many of them, and nothing to boast about. . . . Mostly the planet is a dunghole. Earthmen often wish they could uncover their early ancestors, and bring them to life again, and then throttle them. For their selfishness. For their lack of concern for the generations to come. They filled the world with themselves and used everything up."[7]

Thus Silverberg's novel of a far-flung alien world is not only a narrative exercise in sociology and psychology but also a commentary on contemporary concerns regarding ecology and overpopulation.

Yet if *A Time of Changes* occasionally preaches to the reader —especially in its conclusion, in which Kinnall directly addresses his readers, encouraging them to open themselves to others in love—at times Silverberg through the novel offers less critical views of human nature. For example, Schweiz critiques Earth and those who all but destroyed it, but he also says that humanity began seeding the stars not only as a means of escape but also because they possessed "a hunger to see strange things, a hunger to undertake journeys, a hunger to make fresh starts. To create new and better worlds of man." The context for these aspirations as Schweiz presents them is clearly secular. After noting his own religious skepticism and saying he is fine with this most of the time, he explains his religious longings in terms typical of a scientific worldview common to contemporary science fiction, using the impersonal third person of Kinnall's world:

> One feels the impact of knowing one is entirely alone in the universe. Naked under the stars. . . . No one to offer a hiding place, no one to pray to, do you see? . . . There isn't anyone. You've convinced yourself that no one exists who can give comfort. One wants some system of belief, one wants to submit, to get down and kneel, to be governed by metaphysics, you know? To believe, to have faith! And one can't. And that's when the terror sets in.[8]

Thus Schweiz is driven to this world's drug that offers temporary communion with another human being, a transcendence of self that is mystical in nature. Ultimately Schweiz's critique of religion is validated by Kinnall and by the novel itself, which suggests that in a godless universe, all we have is each other.

This is not to say that this represents Silverberg's final statement on religion, which is dealt with more directly in another 1971 work, his story "Good News from the Vatican." Here an assemblage of laity and clergy, both Catholic and Jewish, await the election of a new pope, who turns out to be a robot. The story raises a number of fascinating issues, from the question of whether intelligent machines would have religious faith to the status of religion in an increasingly secular society to fears people have harbored about their machines.

The fact that the temporary communion of souls in *A Time of Changes* is achieved through the use of drugs in this novel of the early 1970s has led some critics to find the novel dated. For instance, Edgar L. Chapman says that "the 1971 Nebula Award for *A Time of Changes* must now strike many as the judges' bow to the romanticism about hallucinatory drugs in the era of Woodstock (1969) and the Age of Aquarius."[9] Despite Chapman's claim that this is one of the weakest of Silverberg's novels,[10] however, it is worth reading for Silverberg's accomplishments in world building and for his characterization in the context of this world.

Another interesting aspect of *A Time of Changes* concerns its commentary on the nature of civilization. In addition to the novel's treatment of how civilization can corrupt individuals and socialize them in ways contrary to their own best interests and desires, Silverberg through his depiction of the "barbaric" inhabitants of the southern continent shows, as did Niven in *Ringworld,* how civilization can be lost and societies can revert to an earlier state. Thus the novel comments further on how progress is not inevitable, as both Kinnall's culture and the southern continent depict future humans living in ways that seem more historical than futuristic.

History is also a preoccupation of Philip José Farmer's Riverworld series, begun in 1971 with the Hugo Award–winning *To Your Scattered Bodies Go* (1971).[11] Here Farmer combines elements of the historical novel with science fiction, both futuristic and prehistoric. The protagonist is Sir Richard Burton, the famous (some would say infamous) nineteenth-century British explorer and translator. However, Burton's exploits here are even more exotic than those he described in his writings. The novel begins with strangeness and disorientation: Burton dies in 1890 but is instantly revived in a vast featureless space, where he is surrounded by countless other people. Floating in this great blankness, he attempts to resist whatever unseen force holds him in stasis, only to be rendered unconscious. When he again comes to, he experiences what he and others reborn with him eventually term "Resurrection Day."

Along with a multitude of others, Burton is reborn along the shore of an apparently endless river, naked and restored to early adulthood. Eventually these resurrected humans figure out that the metallic canisters they find strapped to their wrists can be "charged" at the large mushroom-shaped devices called "grailstones" spaced a mile apart along the river's shore, thereby supplying them with food and eventually other supplies. Otherwise, the reborn humans have no clue as to why they have been restored to life after their deaths on Earth. Instead, survival becomes paramount. Burton possesses a natural advantage here, given his adventurous experiences on Earth and his linguistic abilities, which helps him communicate easily with the vast variety of people he encounters. Farmer suggests that natural leaders on Earth become leaders on the Riverworld, for as the stars and the nature of this world indicate, they are no longer on Earth. Eventually, Burton's innate curiosity and his fierce independence lead him to chafe against the restrictions imposed by this world and to probe the mystery behind it.

Thus *To Your Scattered Bodies Go* embodies both historical and science fiction elements. The nineteenth-century Burton allies himself with a wide cast of characters, ranging from a prehistoric subhuman to citizens of the late twentieth century (when, apparently, some great catastrophe ended human history) to a sentient alien; while he takes other lovers, he is drawn to a fellow Briton of the 1800s named Alice Hargreaves, the inspiration for Lewis Carroll's Alice fantasies. Burton's chief nemesis is the infamous Nazi Hermann Göring. Thus Farmer's concept cleverly brings together figures from a variety of historical (and prehistoric) periods and even from the future, forcing them to interact in what begins as a level playing field.

What levels the field is the alien environment into which they are thrown, with memories intact but with none of the accoutrements of their lives on Earth except those provided by the grailstones. Apart from this and the controlled environment, they find themselves in a state of nature, and this part of the novel fits into a branch of science fiction more commonly explored by earlier British writers such as H. G. Wells and William Golding, namely, the investigation of life as survival, a return to a preindustrial state. However, this is a state made by an intelligent force rather than a natural one, which takes the novel into the more conventional area of futuristic science fiction. Besides the grailstones and the controlled climate, it becomes clear to Burton, the only one who can recall the intermediate stasis between death and rebirth, that they are part of some scientific experiment conducted by a greater intelligence.

It is also worth noting that Burton, a skeptic on the Riverworld as on Earth, conceives of this intelligence in purely natural terms as opposed to supernatural, and he employs an attitude toward the situation typical of many science fiction protagonists:

Waking up after death, in this valley by this river, he had been powerless to defend himself against the doubts that existed in every man exposed to an early religious conditioning and to an adult society which preached its convictions at every chance.

Now, seeing the alien approach, he was sure that there was some other explanation for this event than a supernatural one.

There was a physical, a scientific, reason for his being here;
he did not have to resort to Judeo-Christian-Moslem myths
for cause.[12]

Such an attitude, in addition to the science fiction elements that
compose the novel, help to distinguish a work such as *To Your
Scattered Bodies Go* from fantasy. As bizarre as Burton finds his
surroundings, he is determined that there must be a logical solution behind the mystery, a solution he sets out to discover over
the course of the novel. He achieves only a glimpse at such a
solution, setting the stage for the next novels in what would
become Farmer's Riverworld series.

The first of these sequels, *The Fabulous Riverboat*, was also
published in 1971. While Burton is mentioned briefly, the protagonist is another strong personality of the nineteenth century,
Samuel Langhorne Clemens, also known as Mark Twain. The
events of this novel occur some years after those of its predeces-
sor, and those segments of humanity that lived in industrialized
societies prior to their "deaths" have begun to re-create what
technologies they can given the limited resources of the Riverworld. Thus Sam Clemens dreams of building a fabulous riverboat, not only to return to the profession of his youth in a world
where writers have little chance to practice their craft but also,
like Burton, to travel the lengthy river to search out the answer
to the mystery behind humanity's collective resurrection. To
accomplish his goals, he enters into an alliance with King John
of England, a Machiavellian figure whose ends are not as obvious as Clemens's, and the conclusion of the novel promises further developments.

As unusual as it may seem to make the author of *The
Adventures of Huckleberry Finn* the protagonist of a science

fiction novel, like Burton, Clemens is a skeptic and a rationalist, a driven character like many more-traditional science fiction figures. Like Burton, Clemens adapts to the world around him and seeks not only to survive but also to understand. Further, their mutual skepticism is justified here: instead of an afterlife imagined in religious terms, which both historical figures doubted, their fictional avatars are reborn into an afterlife created by a greater intelligence, to be sure, but an intelligence that is physical rather than supernatural, an apparently ancient race that has recorded human lives before human beings even had a history. Thus one of Burton's companions is a prehuman known as Kazz, while Clemens's best friend and frequently needed bodyguard belongs to an even older and unknown race of prehuman giants, a lisping titan with a heart of gold whom Clemens affectionately names Joe Miller.

In addition to their settings and protagonists, *To Your Scattered Bodies Go* and *The Fabulous Riverboat* embody other characteristics common to American SF in the 1970s, specifically their treatment of both broad humanistic concerns and more specific social issues. For example, in *To Your Scattered Bodies Go* there are several conversations about human nature as related to humanity's evolutionary heritage, and contemporary concerns are addressed when Burton learns, from a man of the early twenty-first century, of the type of ecological disasters some predicted when Farmer wrote this novel in the early 1970s. Similarly, although *The Fabulous Riverboat* focuses more on action and less on philosophy or politics, the racial political issues of Farmer's time are reflected in the black nationalist aspirations of Soul City, a rival society to the republic led by Clemens and King John.

Another contemporary issue worth noting in the first two novels of Farmer's Riverworld series is the treatment of women.

When humanity is reduced to a state of nature (albeit abetted by the mysterious forces that have gathered them on this new world), it is men who rise to positions of leadership, and women are often reduced to either chattel slavery or, at best, the companions of the men who protect them. To be fair, the women are often depicted as strong, smart, and courageous, but none of them is a leader. This contrasts with Burton's glimpse of the advanced beings, labeled Ethicals, at the end of *To Your Scattered Bodies Go,* whose men and women lead equally. It is as if, Farmer seems to suggest, women can only be the equals of men in an advanced society. Moreover, a passage about a minor character from *The Fabulous Riverboat* is telling:

> There were many like him, men and women who wanted to work if for no other reason than to kill time. There were doctors who had nothing to do but set an occasional broken bone, printers who had no type to set or paper to use, mailmen with no mail to deliver, smiths with no horses to shoe, farmers with no crops to grow, housewives with no children to raise, the food already cooked, housecleaning done in fifteen minutes and no marketing to do, salesmen with nothing to sell.[13]

To be sure, the divisions in gender roles described here applied to many of the resurrected men and women in this strange world, but it is equally strange that in these works of science fiction, in which Farmer extrapolates into the future, he largely failed to pick up on where the feminism of his own time might lead in decades to come. Of course, he was hardly alone among American science fiction writers in this respect.

Beyond the content of these two books, Farmer's Riverworld series, like Niven's Tales of Known Space, is representative of at least two significant trends in contemporary American science fiction, the series and the shared world. According to Chapman, SF writer and editor Frederik Pohl read the manuscript of an early attempt at the Riverworld concept and suggested that, given the nature of the concept, it would work better as a series than as a single novel.[14] While science fiction series existed prior to the 1960s, the push toward multivolume publications was supported in large measure by the phenomenal success of the paperback edition of Tolkien's three-volume fantasy epic *Lord of the Rings* in the 1960s. This not only led to the development of fantasy trilogies and even longer series in the years to come, but as many readers of fantasy were also readers of science fiction, many writers and publishers became more receptive to the idea of setting a series of novels in the same world, often with the same characters. Related to this phenomenon, though a somewhat later development, was the shared-world concept. Thus Farmer followed the first two novels in the Riverworld series with others, both written by him and farmed out to others.

Like Silverberg's "Good News from the Vatican," another 1971 story, Niven's "Inconstant Moon," is set in the near future rather than the more stereotypical distant-future outer space of Farmer's Riverworld books or Niven's own *Ringworld.* "Inconstant Moon," in fact, must have been taken by its initial readers as very near future indeed, given contemporary references to such things as recent moon landings and Johnny Carson's hosting *The Tonight Show.* In its hard-science approach, it resembles Niven's *Ringworld;* in its earthbound, 1970s setting, it is light-years away.

The only reason "Inconstant Moon" is futuristic at all is that the events of the story had not yet happened; there is, for example, a clever reference to *Apollo 19* (*Apollo 17,* in December 1972, was the last in the program). Otherwise, much of the story is indistinguishable in content from anything one could have read in mainstream magazines of the period, with its world of cars and California freeways, war in Vietnam and Cambodia, the Berlin Wall, and apartheid in South Africa, along with its casual assumption of equality between the story's young male protagonist and his girlfriend and its equally casual references to their premarital sex life aided by birth control.

Yet despite its contemporary feel, the story is science fiction. What makes it so is the unusual brightness of the moon. Like many science fiction protagonists, the man here is a problem solver, and initially he hypothesizes that the uncanny lunar illumination is the result of the sun going nova, that he has been spared from destruction only temporarily by being on the dark side of the earth, the rotation of which will in hours make death inevitable. He thus embarks on what he supposes will be his last night in the company of his equally astute girlfriend. However, further evidence renders the nova hypothesis incorrect. Destruction no longer is inevitable, but it still is likely unless they take measures to live through the catastrophe. Thus the story does two things at once, both of them common in science fiction. First, like literary naturalism, to which much science fiction is related in its attitudes about natural law and the indifference of the universe to human affairs, it explores the power of nature in contrast to the relative powerlessness of human beings. In this regard, one of the clear antecedents of "Inconstant Moon" is H. G. Wells's story "The Star" (1897). Second, it exemplifies the survival story, in this case survival in the face of massive disaster.

Several aspects set Niven's story apart from more generic approaches to these familiar story types. Naturally the story is gripping and disturbing, thanks to its plot, but Niven is also strong here when it comes to characterization and dialogue. His main characters are almost stereotypical SF heroes, employing intelligence and scientific knowledge in their stab at survival, but they are believable characters nonetheless, and their relationship and dialogue are presented convincingly (along with curse words, still fairly new in American SF) and charmingly. Like much hard SF of the period, the story is given a somewhat optimistic ending despite the enormous destruction, but Niven makes it seem appropriate.

Reading "Inconstant Moon" today, one is struck by something else. Despite the fact that Niven's story is gripping and well told, it seems dated, a common problem for much science fiction set in the near future. Much like the reader of George Orwell's *Nineteen Eighty-Four* (1949) after 1984, what is one to make of this story set clearly in the 1970s about events that never happened during that decade? One response might be, as Ellen Weil and Gary K. Wolfe note in their book on Niven's contemporary Harlan Ellison, to see the work as disposable, as much pulp fiction was considered when Ellison began his career in the 1950s. Yet "Inconstant Moon" still has power for twenty-first-century readers decades after its initial publication, as does Orwell's *Nineteen Eighty-Four*. It is still worth reading, despite the incongruity between its period and the reality of the reader. Another possible approach, then, would be to consider "Inconstant Moon" as alternate history rather than reading it, as readers at the time would have, as futuristic fiction.[15]

While Niven was a newer writer who had a healthy respect for SF tradition, and while Farmer was a veteran who reinvented himself as science fiction changed around him, the venerable Isaac Asimov, an author whose career began during SF's

Golden Age in the 1930s, also found a new voice in the 1970s, even if his departure from his early work was not as radical as Farmer's or even Silverberg's. This is particularly evident in Asimov's comeback novel, *The Gods Themselves* (1972), which received both the Hugo and the Nebula.

Like many other decades-old SF works, some dating is evident. The human scientists, for example, are all men, and at one point in the story one of them is frustrated by his lack of access to computer time, a realistic concern in the 1970s but no longer one by the 1990s, let alone the novel's setting of the twenty-second century. Also, in his depiction of one of the novel's two alien cultures, he presents a familial relationship of two males and one female in which one of the males is always a Rational and the female is always an Emotional. He does break with convention, however, not only in presenting an unusual three-way relationship but also in the fact that the other male in the triad is always a Parental.

In his nonfiction, Asimov had noted repeatedly in the late 1960s and the early 1970s that he found the experimentation of the New Wave incompatible with his understanding of the genre and his approaches to writing, yet despite this attitude he found himself unable to write much new fiction during this period. *The Gods Themselves* marks a return of sorts, and the novel is noteworthy for how it both shows that Asimov was indeed the same writer in the 1970s that he had been in the 1950s and that he nonetheless had been affected by the New Wave even if he was never a part of it. His depiction of an alien ménage à trois, complete with homoerotic scenes between the two males, marks an interesting departure from his earlier fiction, in which sex of any sort is conspicuously absent. Also, there is some minor experimentation with structure. Part 1 begins with chapter 6, then reverts to chapters 1 and following, with continuations of chapter 6 interspersed among them. All Asimov is doing, however, is beginning the novel in medias res, then employing a series of flashbacks and expositions until finally returning to the present. Similarly, in his presentation of an alien culture of triadic "soft ones" in part 2, the chapters are divided into three sections (1a, 1b, 1c, etc.), each focused on a different member of the triad. This is a clever way of reflecting content through structure, yet Asimov could just as easily have numbered the chapters normally with little diminution of effect.

Another reflection of more recent concerns in Asimov's work comes in the novel's meditations on contemporary matters. The plot deals with physical exchanges between our future world and a parallel universe with somewhat different physical laws that provide free, clean energy for both worlds but that some characters fear could bring devastating changes to their respective universes. On Earth, one such character approaches an influential senator about his fears, and the senator responds:

> It is a mistake . . . to suppose that the public wants the environment protected or their lives saved and that they will be grateful to any idealist who will fight for such ends. What the public wants is their own individual comfort. We know that well enough from our experience in the environmental crisis of the twentieth century.[16]

Here Asimov evinces some concerns about the environment, certainly a frequent topic in New Wave SF, and he touches on a central theme of the novel, human stupidity and the delusional belief in human superiority. There also is more sexual content than in his previous fiction, a reflection of the genre's changing treatment of such matters.

In other ways, the novel is rather traditional. Like Niven's *Ringworld*, *The Gods Themselves* in many ways is an example of hard science fiction, replete with extensive amounts of atomic physics explaining the exchanges with the parallel universe that drive the story. Further, his style is typical of the Golden Age SF writers of a previous generation rather than of the self-conscious stylistic experimentation of the New Wave. An exchange between two of the human characters is representative:

> Bronowski's soft face looked unwontedly grim. "You may be right."
>
> "I know I'm right," said Lamont, just as grimly.[17]

To be fair, not all of Asimov's prose is so wooden, and more commonly he achieves what might be called an invisible style. At any rate, his stylistic conservatism contrasts with the stylistic experimentation found in much SF of the period.

One of the aspects of *The Gods Themselves* that has garnered considerable praise is its depiction of its aliens, a common science fiction subject that rarely appears in Asimov's work. The "soft ones" are truly alien, biologically and culturally different from human beings. As Joseph F. Patrouch Jr. notes, the novel's second section "is a detailed study of consciousness as it developed and lives in a vastly different environment from our own. Perhaps, as much as anything else, it leaves behind an awe-full respect for life and sentience."[18] Donald M. Hassler adds to this assessment, stating that Asimov's work "is hard science-fiction extrapolation at its best because the aliens seem plausible in their own amoebic, energy-starved reality and also suggestive to the reader of what it seems like to be human."[19] Similarly, though it returns to human characters, the third section of the novel is interesting for its careful and imaginative depiction of life as it might be lived on a lunar colony.

The Gods Themselves is also noteworthy for its depiction of its human characters. Those who know little about science fiction often suppose that the genre glorifies science and scientists, and indeed Asimov is clearly a supporter of science. His scientists in this novel, however, are hardly supermen; rather, they can be selfish, petty, and cruel. More sympathetic is the scientist who is the focus of the novel's third section, which not only concludes the story's tensions but also delivers a touching tale of love and redemption in the process.

If Asimov is sociological in his presentation of humans and aliens in *The Gods Themselves,* Ursula K. Le Guin is anthropological in her early science fiction, particularly in her Hainish novels and stories of the late 1960s and early 1970s. One of the most successful writers, both critically and commercially, to emerge from this period, Le Guin gained attention with three novels—*Rocannon's World* (1966), *Planet of Exile* (1966), and *City of Illusions* (1967)—sharing a common historical framework. She then took American SF by storm with the fourth novel in this series, *The Left Hand of Darkness* (1969), which received both the Hugo and the Nebula. A brilliantly conceived work that draws upon her knowledge of anthropology to relate a story of an envoy who encounters a hermaphroditic alien race and rethinks his human preconceptions about sexuality and culture, *The Left Hand of Darkness* is one of the masterpieces of the field.[20]

Another work in the Hainish series, which as a whole develops a vast story about the diverse planets seeded with life by the ancient inhabitants of Hain, is Le Guin's Hugo Award–winning novella *The Word for World Is Forest* (1972), first published in *Again, Dangerous Visions,* edited by Harlan Ellison, and published separately in 1976. In this story, human characters encounter a significantly alien world and are changed by the experience with an otherness that is nonetheless human. But they are not changed in the same way, and Le Guin comes close to stereotype in her depiction of both her humans and her aliens. For instance, one of the humans is a scientist who simply wishes to understand the alien race, while another is a textbook example of the worst stereotypes about military arrogance. The aliens here are also rather two-dimensional "noble savages" who live in harmony with nature, as opposed to the humans who wish to exploit it. Various critics have pointed out that some of Le Guin's work, like some science fiction in general, has a tendency to preach to the reader, and this is to some extent true of *The Word for World Is Forest.*

Also, in its treatment of the damage done to the inhabitants of an idyllic world by human colonists, *The Word for World Is Forest* can be read as an allegorical statement about American involvement in the Vietnam War. While Le Guin is careful to depict a variety of attitudes among the soldiers and officers depicted in the story, the main military figure is obviously the villain, and a stereotypical one at that. Given the nature of the atrocities he and other members of the military practice against the native race, it is not hard to see this novella as an indictment against American military actions in Vietnam. Readers' reactions to this fact may vary. Some may see this as part of what makes science fiction interesting; along with other examples of popular culture, SF can often be read as a reflection of its period, as a way to examine contemporary cultural concerns as they are embodied in works intended for a popular audience. Or this could be read as the author's expression of her own political views through her work, a fact that could be either celebrated or deplored depending upon one's aesthetic and political assumptions.

Le Guin's other widely acknowledged masterpiece besides *The Left Hand of Darkness* is also part of the Hainish series. In *The Dispossessed* (1974), Le Guin combines her lucid, elegant prose with a compelling dual story of two worlds, one poor but politically egalitarian, the other wealthy but highly competitive, oppressive, and patriarchal. Shevek, a young physicist, has been raised on the moon Annares, which was colonized by anarchist revolutionaries from the moon's planet, Urras. He is on the verge of a breakthrough that could radically change interplanetary communication, but in the process of pursuing this breakthrough, he engages in his own form of communication between worlds, traveling to Urras as a visiting scientist. He is amazed at the difference, but also appalled, and eventually he engages in his own form of political rebellion.

It is important to note that, unlike the simple dichotomy between good natives and bad colonizers in *The Word for World Is Forest,* the contrast between the two worlds in *The Dispossessed* is subtle and sophisticated. There are obviously many ways in which life on the anarchistic Annares is superior to that on capitalist Urras: one is almost always assured of work and of life's basic needs, women are the equals of men, and children are cared for. But people on Annares have little leisure, unlike many on Urras, shortages sometimes happen, "partners" (marriage has been abolished on Annares) can be assigned different posts half a world away, and parents typically do not form lifelong relationships with their children. Hence the novel's subtitle, *An Ambiguous Utopia*. The subtitle itself, in fact, is ambiguous, as both worlds could be called "ambiguous utopias." But this phrase especially applies to Annares, as its founders realized that a "perfect" society was an impossibility, that change rather than stasis should always be accepted. Thus, in questioning certain aspects of his own society, in many ways Shevek is the perfect citizen of his world.

In addition to its exploration of scientific theories and of different political, social, and economic models, *The Dispossessed* is also a remarkable work for its impressive literary qualities. One of these is point of view. Almost the entire novel is presented through Shevek's perspective, and for all of his brilliance, he comes across as fully human, with weaknesses and flaws that make him a believable character who struggles to do the right thing in a variety of circumstances. Another is structure: the novel begins in the present, with Shevek leaving Annares for Urras, and then in alternating chapters Le Guin presents readers with his personal history and his experiences on Urras, until the two narrative strands meet in the present with Shevek returning to his home world. Through this combination of point of view and plot structure, readers are led through both the personal and the political, between Annares and Urras, and the interactions between these different strands add to the overall effect of the novel.

"The Day before the Revolution," also published in 1974 but not as part of the novel, is Le Guin's coda of sorts to *The Dispossessed*. It depicts Odo, the guiding force behind the revolution that eventually led to the colonization of Annares, at the end of her life, reflecting on her life as revolution is about to break out. Unlike in *The Dispossessed*, there is little treatment of politics here. Instead, like the novel's depiction of Shevek, this is a character study, a moving depiction of an elderly woman facing death that just happens to be set in a science fiction context. In this regard, "The Day before the Revolution," along with other SF stories with well-developed characters, should put the lie to the frequent charge of critics outside the field that science fiction cannot possibly be considered as literature because it focuses on ideas rather than characters. Even if the assumption that literature is concerned primarily with character is true—and many would say that this assumption is based on prevailing practices in modern fiction rather than on self-evident truths about the nature of literature—there are certainly a number of works in contemporary American science fiction that fulfill this criterion.

Utopian concerns are also evident in a Hugo-winning and frequently anthologized story collected with "The Day before the Revolution" and others in Le Guin's *Wind's Twelve Quarters* (1979), "The Ones Who Walk Away from Omelas" (1973). In it, she posits a world dependent for its utopian existence upon the suffering of the few—another ambiguous utopia. Less character driven than *The Dispossessed* or "The Day before the Revolution," this story is more typical of science fiction in its emphasis on idea, even to the point of becoming allegorical. After all, Le Guin suggests, the idea of the few suffering for the benefit of the many may sound horrifying when taken to such an extreme, but how different is this from the world that we know? In this way, "The Ones Who Walk Away from Omelas," like Le Guin's depiction of Urras in *The Dispossessed,* is a critique of social and economic disparities from a science fiction angle that nonetheless resonates with life in the late-twentieth-century United States.

While Le Guin became the most celebrated of the newer writers to emerge from the 1960s, imbuing American SF with a highly stylized sense of intelligence and emotional depth and fueling the trend toward more women reading and writing science fiction, she was far from the only writer helping to change the face of the field.

Along with Le Guin, one of the best SF authors of either gender to emerge in the United States from the late 1960s was Joanna Russ. Although Le Guin dealt with gender issues in works such as *The Left Hand of Darkness* and *The Dispossessed,* her work during this period was not overtly feminist, unlike that of Russ, as is evident in such well-crafted works as Russ's Nebula Award–winning story "When It Changed," first published in Ellison's *Again, Dangerous Visions,* and her brilliant and challenging novel *The Female Man* (1975). "When It Changed" takes place on the planet Whileaway, which after a plague that killed only the men is inhabited solely by women, who have learned how to reproduce with one another and have established a utopian but realistically down-to-earth community. When a group of male space travelers arrives, they come in as if they are here to rescue the damsels in distress, but the women's response, apart from curiosity at seeing men for the first time in centuries, is essentially, Rescued from what?

Whileaway also figures in the intertwining stories of *The Female Man,* although it is presented as a possible future Earth rather than another planet. Here Russ artfully weaves together four narrative strands representing different potential realities, along with witty asides, postmodern commentary, and the occasional lecture. The narratives involve Janet, the main character in "When It Changed"; Jael, who comes from another possible future in which men and women are at war;[21] Joanna, whose reality is that of the 1970s United States of the reader's reality; and Jeannine, who lives in an alternate present with a different history, in which the Great Depression continues and World

War II never occurred. Through exploring these different possible realities and bringing them into juxtaposition, Russ analyzes relationships between the sexes as well as between individuals and society from a variety of perspectives, creating in the process a complex, compelling work of art.

Part of what makes *The Female Man* so compelling as a work of fiction, apart from its adroit juggling of satire and straight SF and its experimental narrative techniques, is its realistic depiction of what it is like to navigate the emotional minefields of romantic relationships, an aspect of the novel that is little commented upon in comparison with its literary style or its examination of feminist ideas made concrete. In her presentation of Janet's tentative declaration of her love for her wife, in the repressed attraction between Janet and the adolescent Laura Rose of Joanna's reality as they embark upon a forbidden affair (forbidden for Laura Rose because of what she has been taught about lesbianism being wrong, for Janet because Laura Rose is younger), and in Jeannine's agonizing vacillations as passive love object in a patriarchal society, Russ's exploration of the joys and anxieties associated with romantic love is one of the best to be found in contemporary American literature, science fiction or otherwise.

Given the book's radical nature, both as a science fiction novel and as feminist fiction, it is not surprising that Russ experienced some difficulty in getting the work published; in fact, it passed among Russ's friends in typescript for a few years prior to its publication. Part of what may have made some SF publishers uncomfortable with the book was its overt feminist tone, which would also have been true of many mainstream publishers in the early 1970s, but also its frank depiction of sex. American science fiction, which historically had been almost puritanical in its use of sexual content despite using titillating illustrations of nearly naked women for decades during the magazine era, was slower than other types of literature to become more sexually explicit; and even while these taboos were challenged by selected writers as early as the 1950s and by many more in the late 1960s and early 1970s, many SF publishers would have balked at the sex scenes in *The Female Man*. The presentation of lesbian sex is actually rather tame, though of course some readers would be offended merely at the suggestion of two women making love; but the scene in which Jael enjoys sex with an android man is explicit indeed, far more than most contemporary readers were accustomed to in the genre.

Russ, who like Le Guin and their contemporary Samuel R. Delany has also been a provocative critic of SF, is not alone in using SF for feminist projects.[22] In Suzy McKee Charnas's *Walk to the End of the World* (1974), for instance, she depicts a post-disaster world in which men rule and consider women responsible for the near-destruction of the planet and good only for breeding more men. A woman named Alldera escapes from the patriarchal Holdfast into the wilderness, and in the sequel, *Motherlines* (1978), she discovers different matriarchal societies that, though they are hardly utopian, are considerable improvements upon the one she escaped.[23]

Besides Le Guin and Russ, one of the most significant female writers of this period was an author who initially hid her gender behind a male pseudonym: James Tiptree Jr., who was eventually revealed to be Alice Sheldon. Women writing as men in male-dominated markets was nothing new, but Sheldon, who had worked for the CIA, so successfully crafted a male persona for herself that the science fiction community generally believed that Tiptree was a man, and in fact arguments were presented to that effect. As Amanda Boulter notes in her perceptive analysis of how knowing or not knowing Tiptree's gender affects the reading of his/her work, Tiptree "had not only 'passed' as a man but had been described as the most masculine of all science fiction writers."[24] In retrospect, both Sheldon's successful presentation of herself as a male writer and, more important, her fiction challenge a wide variety of attitudes about gender, and it is fitting that the Tiptree Award is given for works that do the same.

A particularly telling Tiptree story in this regard is "The Women Men Don't See" (1973). The male narrator, who at first barely notices the mother and daughter with whom he shares an airplane on an expedition in South America, is very much from the hard-boiled school of American fiction, almost a parody of Ernest Hemingway's characters. But after the plane crashes, he is continually forced to revise his views of the women as he witnesses the mother's cool competence and the daughter's seduction of their native pilot. For most of the story, the situation is realistic, but it turns science fictional once aliens enter the picture. This in itself is worth noting: if a reader picks up the story with no notion of Tiptree being a science fiction writer or of the story being science fiction, he or she will likely read the story as a realistic mainstream work then have that perception jarred when the aliens appear. In contrast, if a reader knows that Tiptree is a science fiction writer or that the story is science fiction, he or she will read through the first two-thirds or so of the story anticipating just when the SF element is going to appear. Just as knowing or not knowing the author's gender affects the reading, so does knowing or not knowing in advance that this is a work of science fiction.

Like other well-known Tiptree stories (such as "The Girl Who Was Plugged In" and "Houston, Houston, Do You Read?"),

"The Women Men Don't See" is a cutting examination of gender issues. One of the story's two major twists is that the women, both examples of "the women men don't see," decide to accompany the alien scientists when they return to their planet. Perhaps, the mother suggests, they will feel less alien among the aliens than in a man's world.

Another young woman men do not see was the title character of a very different kind of work published a year later, Stephen King's *Carrie* (1974). This first novel by a writer who would soon become one of the best-selling authors in history is commonly credited with helping to lead a revival in horror fiction in the United States, and indeed it is a horror novel; but as Peter Nicholls notes, horror is "a genre defined not by its content but by its presumptive effect," and in content *Carrie* and quite a few other horror novels by King and company are science fiction.[25] In *Carrie,* for instance, an unpopular adolescent girl terrorized by both her classmates and her religiously fanatical mother develops telekinetic powers. The situations depicted in the novel lead to the emotional effects of horror, but the abilities that Carrie possesses and eventually employs are pure science fiction.

Horror of another sort was experienced in the early 1970s and earlier in the Vietnam War, and Le Guin was not the only writer to address this through the lens of science fiction. It is perhaps fitting that the most significant SF work to touch on Vietnam was written by a veteran of the conflict, Joe Haldeman. The war, in which he served as a combat engineer from 1967 to 1969 and in which he was wounded, is clearly the context of Haldeman's powerful novel *The Forever War* (1974). In some ways a response to Robert A. Heinlein's enthusiastically militaristic *Starship Troopers* (1959), *The Forever War* deals with an interstellar war between humans and aliens with a hive mentality. Haldeman effectively describes the military training of the soldiers and the occasional experience of combat. As he traces the military career of his main character, who advances from private to major, he also examines through his first-person narrator how warfare is experienced at different levels of the hierarchy. Haldeman portrays the alienating effects of warfare through the time dilation the soldiers experience as they travel through space; since the collapsars that jump them from one part of the universe to another and their travels near the speed of light make the war seem only ten years long for the soldiers, though it has lasted a thousand years, they are in effect cut off from the civilization for which they fight. It would over-simplify Haldeman's accomplishment in the novel to reduce it to a metaphor for American military involvement in Vietnam, but the echoes of the recent war are present in the future war he describes.

Along with the novel's convincing treatment of how technology might affect the conduct of war in the next millennium, *The Forever War* is also a fascinating example of future history. The protagonist, William Mandella, and his girlfriend, both of them soldiers, periodically visit Earth between their stints in the service, and they find things radically changed there, just as SF readers experience a radical difference between their world and the worlds presented to them in science fiction. Future shock becomes literal for these characters, whose visits to their home planet are spaced decades or even centuries apart. Through these visits, Haldeman effectively presents readers with a potential future history that is at once shocking and seemingly plausible. For example, after his training and first combat experience, Mandella returns home. Although in his experience only a few years have passed, on Earth it has been twenty-six years since his last visit. His middle-aged mother is now elderly, his father has died, and there are other changes:

> She took my cape and hustled me into the living room of the suite, where I got a real shock: my father was standing there, smiling but serious, inevitable pipe in his hand. I felt a flash of anger at the army for having misled me—then realized he couldn't be my father, looking as he did, the way I remembered him from childhood.
>
> "Michael? Mike?"
>
> He laughed. "Who else, Willy?" My kid brother, quite middle-aged. . . .
>
> The three of us sat down around a marble coffee table and Mother passed around joints.[26]

Even more changes are in store for Mandella down the road, a few years (for him) or centuries (for Earth) later:

> "Wait. You mean nobody . . . everybody in my company is homosexual? But me?"
>
> "William, everybody on Earth is homosexual. Except for a thousand or so; veterans and incurables."
>
> "Ah." What could I say? "Seems like a drastic way to solve the population problem."
>
> "Perhaps. It does work, though; Earth's population is stable at just under a billion. When one person dies or goes off-planet, another is quickened."
>
> "Not 'born.'"
>
> "Born, yes, but not the old-fashioned way. Your old term for it was 'test-tube babies,' but of course they don't use a test-tube."
>
> "Well, that's something."

"Part of every creche is an artificial womb that takes care of a person the first eight or ten months after quickening. What you would call birth takes place over a period of days; it isn't the sudden, drastic event it used to be."

O brave new world, I thought. . . .

. . . "Yourself, you, uh . . . are you homosexual?"

"Oh, no," he said. I relaxed. "Actually, though, I'm not hetero any more, either." He slapped his hip and it made an odd sound. "Got wounded and it turned out that I had a rare disorder of the lymphatic system, can't regenerate. Nothing but metal and plastic from the waist down. To use your word, I'm a cyborg."

Far out, as my mother used to say.[27]

Experiences such as this are as jarring for the protagonist as for the reader, ironically giving the soldiers more in common with their supposed enemy than with the civilization for which they believe they are fighting. Eventually it is their fellow humans who are alien to them.

Transformed societies are also central to Katherine Mac-Lean's 1975 *Missing Man* and Samuel R. Delany's *Triton* (1976). *Missing Man* is an example of what science fiction scholars refer to as a "fix-up novel," a work that has its origin in a number of shorter pieces, typically published separately in magazines, that are "fixed up" to form a novel. At times the result can be effective, as in Walter M. Miller Jr.'s science fiction masterpiece *A Canticle for Leibowitz* (1959), but MacLean's book is more obviously an assemblage of related pieces fused together into a not-quite-organic unity. Even so, the novel is interesting in several ways, and the novella *The Missing Man,* which is incorporated into the novel, received the Nebula Award in 1971.

Set in 1999, the novel depicts a near-future New York City that is both familiar and transformed. While there are significant technological developments that make the city futuristic, there are also large green spaces in the city, other than the parks, many of them within the enclosed communes of like-minded folks who band together. The protagonist, who narrates the novel except for some awkward transitions to a third-person narrator when he is unconscious, struggles to make his way in this transformed society. He possesses extrasensory perception (ESP) and eventually works for the Rescue Squad, helping to find people in trouble or those about to commit crimes, similar to characters in Philip K. Dick's story "The Minority Report" (1956), the basis for Steven Spielberg's 2002 movie *Minority Report*. Another connection with earlier SF comes with the repeated use of the verb "grok" from Robert A. Heinlein's *Stranger in a Strange Land*.

MacLean's *Missing Man* employs its depiction of a future New York and of ESP in a largely episodic, action-filled plot, but it offers some commentary on ethnic and political divisions, youth movements, and society. However, just as she fails to integrate the different stories and novellas into a seamless novel, MacLean offers an odd combination of SF thriller, police procedural, psychological novel, and philosophical dialogue on personal freedom versus social norms and goals. Her treatment of what it might be like to have ESP is interesting, and many of the ideas presented in the novel are intriguing, but as a whole the novel lacks a sense of unity. Also, as often happens with science fiction, some details help to make the work somewhat dated: she envisions a world in which vending machines accept credit cards and some people live in underwater domed cities, but office workers still use typewriters and carbon paper—much like, in

Ursula K. Le Guin's *Dispossessed* (1974), Cetian physicists take interstellar flight for granted but still use slide rules.

At the conclusion of *The Forever War*, Mandella is presented with a host of choices about where to go next, as different lifestyle choices are readily accepted on a number of worlds colonized by humans. This concept is the focus of Samuel R. Delany's *Triton*, a challenging, complex novel that is one of the more self-consciously literary examples of SF between 1970 and 1976.

Delany, very much associated with the New Wave, drew heavily upon structuralist ideas in several of his works of the late 1960s and the 1970s, including *Dhalgren* (1975) and *Triton*, both of which unite space-opera elements, imaginative extrapolations of future societies, and abstruse philosophizing. Perhaps more than any other American SF writer of the period, Delany strove to create in his work literary artifacts that testified, like much postmodern fiction at the time, to their own nature as constructions of language. Many of Delany's works, for all their SF trappings, are really more about the nature of language, literature, and art than about traditional SF subjects.

In *Triton*,[28] Delany deals with several traditional SF themes, both old (the human conquest of space, speculations about technological development and future social structures) and new (alternate sexualities situated within a variety of social and political contexts), yet the novel is very much an exploration of expression, linguistic and artistic as well as personal. The style of the novel could best be described as impressionistic, and in this sense *Triton*, like so many New Wave works, could be seen as an example of SF's late appropriation of modernist technique; moreover, in certain ways the plot of the novel echoes that of Virginia Woolf's experimental *Orlando*.

It should also be noted that in *Triton,* Delany, who also has written a substantial amount of SF criticism, is undoubtedly contributing to a fictional conversation with other SF writers, in particular Russ and Le Guin, concerning topics such as gender and utopia. *Triton* has much in common with Russ's *Female Man* in its exploration of gender identity and sexuality, as Delany's macho protagonist searches for his true nature in a society in which essentially anything goes and even gender and sexual preference are not set in stone. In addition, the subtitle of *Triton, An Ambiguous Heterotopia,* obviously echoes the subtitle of Le Guin's *Dispossessed, An Ambiguous Utopia,* as does Delany's exploration of a person's relationship to a society that strives toward perfection (although this is defined differently in the two novels).

This type of conversation, which is also evident in the ways in which Haldeman's *Forever War* is clearly a critique of Heinlein's *Starship Troopers,* is typical of much of the better science fiction published in the United States and elsewhere in which challenging ideas are treated seriously through the medium of fiction and in which authors are to some extent in dialogue with one another. In so doing, authors walk a fine line between successfully incorporating ideas into effective works of fiction and preaching to their readers and thus letting the quality of the fiction suffer, a charge frequently made against much utopian literature, to which SF is generically related, and against Heinlein's late novels published in the 1970s and 1980s. However, the notion of SF as a literature of ideas, frequently used as a defense of the form against its less-informed critics, only goes so far, as certainly many SF stories and novels are short on ideas (not to mention characterization and style) and long on good old-fashioned adventure. And some writers, such as Le Guin, Haldeman, and Delany, manage to do it all well.

Utopian considerations of another sort are the subject of "Strange Wine" (1976), a story by Harlan Ellison, another author who has sought to infuse his work with literary qualities beyond what had earlier been typical of much American SF. The story concerns a man who believes he has not always been a human being, but is an alien. Deeply depressed, he believes that he has been sent to Earth from his native planet for some terrible transgression that he cannot recall; indeed, he can barely remember anything of his previous life. In despair, he takes his life, only to be resurrected in his true form on his home world. Thus he learns that his feeling of alienation on Earth was genuine. Nevertheless, he was mistaken: his sojourn on Earth was not punishment for a crime but a reward for having lived a virtuous life. The life that made him so miserable on Earth, he learns, was heavenly in comparison with life on his home planet and indeed anywhere else in the universe. For all its problems, it seems, Earth is the best of all possible worlds. All of this is conveyed in a narrative that effectively combines the intense emotional content typical of Ellison's work with a science fiction framework that provides an ironic comment upon human problems, resulting in a story that is both thought provoking and moving.

The increasing level of literary sophistication and maturity in American SF of the first half of the 1970s is due in part to training: many SF writers of the Golden Age were trained as scientists, while many of the newer writers studied literature in college or at any rate had backgrounds closer to those of other types of writers. At the same time, many SF writers continued to come to the field more as trained scientists than as students of literature, as the emphasis upon hard SF made clear. And in a few years some writers would emerge, such as Gregory Benford and John Kessel, who were equally at home in what C. P. Snow famously termed the "Two Cultures."

Thus the diversity of Delany's Triton is emblematic of the increasing diversity of American SF from 1970 to 1976, that bicentennial year in which the United States reviewed its history and considered its future. From conservatism to liberalism to gradual adaptation to changing times, both political and literary, American SF began to transform itself.

CHAPTER 3

From Science Fantasy to Hard Science Fiction, 1977–1983

Although not all American science fiction published in the first half of the 1970s came from writers influenced by the New Wave, the period nonetheless continued to witness the transition of science fiction into a literary form less isolated and more shaped by notions of literary quality found in mainstream literary fiction. With this in mind, some parallels can be drawn between American SF from the late 1960s to the mid-1970s and American cinema during the same period. Many American filmmakers, influenced by the French cinema's Nouvelle Vague (New Wave) and numerous other sources, engaged in a period of creativity and experimentalism during this "Hollywood renaissance," presenting viewers with daring films such as *Bonnie and Clyde* (1967), *The Graduate* (1967), *The Wild Bunch* (1969), *M*A*S*H* (1970), *The Godfather* (1972) and *The Godfather II* (1974), *Chinatown* (1974), and *Taxi Driver* (1976), along with the science fiction classics *2001: A Space Odyssey* (1968) and *A Clockwork Orange* (1971), both adapted by Stanley Kubrick from British works. As in the 1930s, American cinema experienced a golden age during one of the country's worst periods. In this case, it produced a series of artistically conceived, unconventional films at a time when the nation was struggling through the Vietnam War; social tensions resulting from the civil rights movement, the second wave of American feminism, and the incipient gay and lesbian rights movement; the Watergate scandal; and the onset of what Jimmy Carter, elected president at the end of 1976, would term a national "malaise."

Given these tensions and those to follow in the late 1970s, such as a national energy crisis and growing concerns about environmental damage, it is perhaps little wonder that American movies and other forms of entertainment, including science fiction, would become increasingly escapist, as indeed were many movies of the 1930s and much of the fiction produced during the Great Depression. In the mid-1970s, movie audiences were exposed to not only challenging films directed by people such as Francis Ford Coppola and Martin Scorsese but also less-challenging fare directed by other members of what is called the "film school generation," such as Steven Spielberg and his friend George Lucas, much of which drew upon science fiction themes. For instance, Spielberg's *Jaws* (1975), which film historians generally label as the first modern blockbuster, is essentially a monster movie, while his *Close Encounters of the Third Kind* deals with first contact between aliens and humans, as does his *E.T. the Extra-Terrestrial* (1982). The latter two films, along with the success of Richard Donner's *Superman* (1978) and especially of Lucas's *Star Wars* films, the first of which was released in 1977, led to a resurgence of interest in science fiction on the big screen not seen since the 1950s.

Response to these films among science fiction readers and writers was mixed. While special effects had advanced considerably with films such as *2001: A Space Odyssey* and *Star Wars* and continued to advance year by year, thus enabling filmmakers to present visions of SF ideas more convincingly than ever before, the kinds of SF films that tended to be made when science fiction on the big screen became popular again leaned heavily on spectacle and less so on ideas (not to mention characterization and dialogue). Action and adventure were more likely to draw audiences, it seemed to filmmakers, than the kinds of attributes possessed by the best written SF. Thus in many ways the boom in science fiction cinema that began in the late 1970s, while visually exciting, was something of a regression to older forms of SF storytelling that American writers had largely left behind decades earlier. Striking evidence to this is the testimony of British SF author and historian Brian W. Aldiss, who was called in as an authority in a case in which the studio that distributed *Star Wars* was suing the studio that made *Battlestar Galactica* (1978) for theft of intellectual property. Aldiss's view was that both films drew from earlier action-adventure SF. When asked about his initial response to *Star Wars,* Aldiss replied, "I experienced the delights of recognition."[1]

While many fans experienced such nostalgia, negative feelings about the science fiction movie boom were plenteous in the SF community. Science fiction in written form had long been judged, as Theodore Sturgeon had claimed, on its worst examples; now came the added fear that written science fiction would be judged to be on a par with the average SF film, with its special effects–driven emphasis on explosions and strange extraterrestrials.

Written SF's relationship to science fiction in the movies or on television also led to two developments. One was tie-ins, the books that were published in conjunction with popular SF movies and television shows, especially the *Star Wars* films and *Star Trek,* already a phenomenon in television syndication and, beginning in the late 1970s, the inspiration for a series of motion pictures. At first these books were devoted to retelling the stories viewers had seen on the big or small screen, but soon both developed formidable franchises, with each series spawning dozens of titles placing familiar characters in new situations. This created something of a conflict for many in the SF community: many readers of these books were also readers of science fiction in general, but many came to these books because of their connections to their favorite movie series or television show and remained content to limit their science fiction reading to these particular books. And while tie-ins were generally written by competent professionals, there was a concern among many in the SF community that these books, in developing the characters and situations from their media inspirations more fully, were actually antithetical to the spirit of science fiction, which was thought to encourage imagination and the consideration of new ideas as opposed to merely more adventures in the same familiar universe. At the same time, there was something hypocritical about this attitude, as written SF itself had a long history of series, sequels, and shared worlds, trends which would only become more prevalent in American SF in the last few decades of the twentieth century.

The second development, in terms of both content and marketing, was the change in the relationship between SF and fantasy. Again, *Star Wars* had something to do with this. *Star Wars* and its sequels have much of the traditional apparatus of science fiction—spaceships, aliens, lasers, space stations, and so on— but in many ways the stories draw more on fantasy motifs than on traditional SF narratives: guided by a wizardly mentor, a young man must rescue a princess from a monster. And in its treatment of the Force, which until Lucas returned to the series in the late 1990s was treated mystically rather than scientifically,

Star Wars verges into the realm of fantasy. Thus the film and its sequels are examples of a hybrid of the two called science fantasy. *Star Wars* did not invent this kind of mixed narrative, which had existed for some time, but it was partially responsible for reviving interest in the possibilities of combining science fiction and fantasy, and such hybrids were not uncommon in American SF from the 1970s on.

But *Star Wars* was not wholly responsible for this phenomenon. Another factor was the increasing popularity of fantasy itself. J. R. R. Tolkien's fantasy novels *The Hobbit* and *Lord of the Rings,* though originally published in Great Britain in 1938 and 1954–55 respectively, were adopted by young readers in the United States in great numbers in the 1960s, and the books' popularity remained steady into the 1970s. American writers and publishers took notice and began reprinting older fantasy stories and producing new ones. Series, especially trilogies (*Lord of the Rings,* though a single novel, was published in three volumes), were particularly popular. Writers were encouraged by the possibility of developing, as Tolkien had, richly detailed, complex worlds populated by numerous characters (the generous view) or saw series as a less-demanding way to make money at their keyboards (the cynical view); publishers saw series as a way to make money (the cynical view, again).

This development affected American science fiction in a few ways. First, as fantasy became an increasingly viable market for new work, many SF writers also worked as fantasy writers, thus making it possible, for better or worse, for more writers to work full time *as* writers. This possibility was aided by the fact that the markets for both SF and fantasy had grown, in books as well as in the magazines that lingered. The negative side to this is the frequent charge leveled at many writers of fantastic fiction that they overproduce. From their perspective, of course, their stories and novels pay the rent and put food on the table. But over-production in SF is related to the concerns regarding media tie-ins: if there are more average or mediocre books out there, and they are selling well for one reason or another, is it possible that a sort of literary Gresham's Law will take effect, that bad books will drive out good ones?

Nevertheless, good books continued to be written in the field, by both younger writers and veterans, who either wrote in much the same style as they had written in the 1950s and 1960s (Isaac Asimov, Robert A. Heinlein, and Frank Herbert) or developed as writers (Philip José Farmer and Frederik Pohl). Perhaps the best example of a veteran writer adopting some of the "newer" literary techniques practiced by the New Wave is Pohl, born in 1919, who began his professional career in SF as a teenager. Approaching sixty, he published what many consider his finest solo novel, *Gateway* (1977), which received all of the field's major awards.[2]

In *Gateway,* Pohl subverts a longstanding tradition in American SF, especially as encouraged by editor John W. Campbell Jr.: the notion that human beings would be superior to any alien race they might encounter, that human ingenuity and morality would reign supreme, and that humanity would one day conquer the stars. Instead, Pohl presents a humbler vision of humanity's place in the universe. A mysterious alien race known as the Heechee has seemingly abandoned dozens of spacecraft on a planetoid known as Gateway. Humans understand little of the technology behind the spacecraft but enough to pilot them wherever they are programmed to go. A Heechee vessel might take a human pilot to a source of lucrative Heechee artifacts—or to death. Pohl was not the first SF author to suggest that humans might play a secondary role in the universe if there are other intelligences in the depths of space, but *Gateway* is one of the best SF novels to use this possibility as a metaphor for the uncertainty of life in an unpredictable world.

Gateway, however, is much more than simply a gold-rush story transposed into science fiction terms. While Pohl in all his work captures the sense of how life might be lived under radically different circumstances—in a Pohl novel, you almost always know how the economy works, how things smell, and from where people get their meals—and while Pohl, here and elsewhere, conveys scientific details and extrapolations clearly and convincingly, this is more than a treatment of life-or-death adventures in outer space. To use a New Wave term, the novel is also concerned with "inner space," specifically, the damaged psyche of the book's protagonist, Robinette "Bob" Broadhead. While taking his chances with the Heechee ships and becoming wealthy in the process, Broadhead falls in love with a woman named Klara.

The loss of Klara plunges Broadhead into despair, and he consults a psychiatrist for help. In this way, *Gateway* differs little from many other narratives in American culture of the late 1970s, which were filled with characters seeking emotional healing or trying to get in touch with themselves on the analyst's couch—as in, for example, a film released the same year as *Gateway*, Woody Allen's *Annie Hall*. The difference here is that Broadhead's psychiatrist is a computer. This particular aspect of the novel is an excellent example of extrapolation, something SF writers often do. Pohl did not invent the idea of a computer psychiatrist, but he took his knowledge of contemporary experiments with computerized therapy and expanded the idea through imagining how this might develop in the future. Yet again there is more going on in Pohl's novel than the presentation of gosh-wow technology. Broadhead's loss and the resulting damage it brings to his life are serious matters, and Pohl's depiction of his psychological crisis is as convincing and moving as any comparable example in mainstream literature. Thus *Gateway* is one of many SF novels that give the lie to the argument often made by mainstream critics who judge science fiction from a position of ignorance, claiming that "science fiction" and "literature" are mutually exclusive categories because literature deals with character (which is not always true even of the classics of the Western tradition) while science fiction is focused on ideas.[3] *Gateway,* contrary to the proclamations of such critics, does both.

However, our hypothetical mainstream critic might ask, what about style? Surely, he or she might say, science fiction falls short of the standards of literature at the stylistic level. Indeed, much science fiction pays little attention to stylistic quality, but this is also true of much mainstream fiction. As is discussed more fully in chapter 6, mainstream critics of science fiction often discuss "science fiction" as it were a homogeneous entity but typically do not do the same with mainstream fiction, which ranges from the most tawdry, stylistically wooden best sellers to the work of Nobel Prize recipients. And when such critics compare science fiction with other types of fiction in terms of quality, they tend to compare the worst of science fiction with the best of mainstream fiction, failing in the process to recognize that science fiction is as diverse in quality as mainstream fiction.

Writers such as Pohl demonstrate that SF authors can be as attuned to matters of style as to ideas and characterization, and one of the pleasures of reading Pohl is that much of his work is sly, satirical, ironic, and very funny, and it is evident that he has given some attention to not just what is being said but also how it is said. Moreover, besides the traditional narrative that runs throughout *Gateway,* Pohl intersperses a variety of other texts, ranging from computer-coded transcripts of Broadhead's psychiatric sessions to an assortment of advertisements (many of them hilarious) to legal contracts, brochures, and other documents. While the novel is hardly experimental in technique, the inserted nonnarrative texts give readers both a broader background on the setting and a different type of reading experience, one reminiscent of certain modernist or postmodernist works.

Thus *Gateway,* about the human exploitation of space via unpredictable technology abandoned by its alien creators, combines Pohl's gifts for satire and for describing the exigencies of everyday life in other environments along with his ability to work complex scientific ideas seamlessly into well-crafted stories with modernist literary techniques. Yet the novel, for all of its intriguing ideas and pointed satires of corporate and individual greed, is also a moving human story of loss and guilt, occasioned by the consequences of the protagonist's actions and the hard facts of physics.[4]

Like *Gateway,* John Crowley's *Engine Summer* (1979) takes a traditional science fiction topic—here a society returned to a more basic mode of life following a global catastrophe rather than the exploration of space, as in Pohl—and provides it with a new perspective. Civilization has been destroyed, and in its place the novel's narrator describes a pastoral world where the survivors, while not exactly utopian, strive to live in harmony with nature. It is, in fact, a world lived in accordance with traditional Native American ideals, although the Indians are long gone, and the title of the novel puns on the phrase "Indian summer," referring to the pleasant weather of late autumn. But this is not exactly a bucolic Eden, and the title carries a double meaning both as it relates to its setting and as it relates to the narrator, Rush that Speaks.

In addition to the novel's depiction of its post-holocaust world, Crowley's narrator is another aspect that has contributed to the book's growing acclaim as an important work of American science fiction (following a lukewarm initial response from fans). In relating the events of his youth and development, Rush that Speaks renders *Engine Summer* a bildungsroman, and his life story is related orally in the hope that he may thereby achieve enlightenment. Here, however, Crowley complicates matters. Eventually it is revealed that the teller of the tale is not a living human being but the electronically preserved personality of a long-dead figure, who both relives his life afresh with each telling and is trapped in it. Consequently, the novel's details take on added significance in the rereading. Thus the quest narrative, another traditional type in science fiction and especially in fantasy, which the book evokes even while remaining steadfastly SF, is turned on its head, as it becomes clear that the story is actually a twice-told tale.

Memory and the meaning of life are consistent themes in Crowley's work. For instance, in his 1985 story "Snow," a wealthy woman has her life recorded by a tiny electronic device called a "wasp," and after her death her husband is able to watch fragments of their life together. However, the company that provides this service can only present these recordings randomly, and their quality degrades over time, thus providing a haunting metaphor for memory and a poignant treatment of loss. Along with "Snow," *Engine Summer* is perhaps Crowley's most sophisticated and developed treatment of memory and the meaning of life. What makes us what we are? Why is the past important to us? How do we live our lives in the face of an uncertain future? These are questions that are movingly explored in the novel. As Brian W. Aldiss and David Wingrove put it, "Rush that Speaks is as intrigued as Crowley's reader by the enigma of the past—that is, of our present selves and why we are as we are."[5] In this way, also, *Engine Summer* anticipates another major American SF work that deals with similar issues, Gene Wolfe's *Book of the New Sun* (1980–83), just as Crowley's setting and his treatment of post-holocaust tribal life anticipates Ursula K. Le Guin's *Always Coming Home* (1985).

Crowley's treatment of memory and time and of the living of an individual life is enhanced by his use of language. Like Wolfe and Le Guin, Crowley is a consummate stylist, and readers and critics often describe his prose as poetic or lyrical. But attention to style alone, or to the novel's self-reflexive structure, does not account for its depth. As with any writer of literature—and *Engine Summer* is indeed a literary work, in the best sense of the term—Crowley combines several facets of fiction, from deft characterization to evocative presentation of setting to thematic and symbolic richness, into a whole that both develops the materials of science fiction and in a sense transcends them.

If the complexity and ambition of Crowley's *Engine Summer* proved daunting or off-putting for traditional readers of science fiction, his accomplishment was nonetheless recognized by many of his peers and by critics. In the science fiction community, it was a runner-up for both the British Science Fiction Award and the John W. Campbell Award; outside SF, it was nominated for the American Book Award in the science fiction category. The fact that in 1980 the American Book Award separated SF and other types of genre fiction from general fiction, however, indicates something of the ongoing ghettoization of the field, and it is noteworthy that Crowley, for all his achievements as a writer, has received limited attention outside the genre. Nor has he proven a popular writer within American SF in terms of sales and the two major awards, the Hugo and the Nebula. It is as if he is too literary an author for the general SF readership and, by virtue of his association with science fiction and fantasy, not literary enough for readers of mainstream literary fiction. Additionally, he has not been as prolific as many of his peers in science fiction and fantasy, fields in which readers and publishers tend to favor those who can produce far more stories and novels than Crowley has written over the course of his career.

In contrast, Octavia E. Butler has managed the rare feat of achieving acclaim both within science fiction and beyond it, due in large part not only to the quality of her work, which is considerable, but also to her provocative treatments of race and gender. Butler's *Kindred* (1979), which of all her novels has gained the largest readership both within and without SF, is very different from either *Gateway* or *Engine Summer*, yet it too uses science fiction to explore a character coming to terms with herself and her past. The character in this case is a young African American woman named Dana, an aspiring writer living in 1976. Without warning, she is transported from contemporary California to what readers soon learn is antebellum Maryland, where she sees a white boy about to drown. She saves the boy's life, but her own life is threatened by the boy's father, at which point she returns to her home, dripping wet. Thus begins Butler's unique twist on an old SF form, the time-travel tale.

Dana has barely recovered from the shock and disorientation of her first time-travel experience when she is again transported to Maryland in the early 1800s. This time she sees a white boy, who looks like the boy she had saved earlier only older, trying to extinguish a fire in his bedroom. Again she saves him, only this time she does not immediately return to her own time. After talking with the boy, she discovers that he is indeed the same child she had saved only moments ago—moments ago, that is, for her; a few years for him. Thus begins Dana's relationship with this boy, Rufus, the son of a small plantation owner in rural Maryland. For some reason that is never revealed, Dana is called back from her own time and place whenever Rufus's life is in danger, which, given his recklessness, occurs more than twice. Also, under the rules that govern this time-travel situation, time passes differently for the two characters: Dana's experiences from her point of view total only a few months, but along the way Rufus grows up into a young man.

What makes *Kindred* an especially striking and powerful novel is not just its time-travel narrative but also the relationship between Dana and Rufus and how this is shaped by the past setting of the novel. Rufus's father is a slave owner, and Dana knows enough about this historical period to understand that, lacking any papers to prove she is not a slave, she could easily be taken into slavery. Up to a point she is aided by her literacy and her historical knowledge, but one of the strong points of the novel, in contrast to other time-travel stories in which the traveler from the future is indisputably superior to those in the past, is that Dana realizes she lacks the knowledge she needs to completely ensure her safety. Thus the threat of slavery is constant during her visits to the past, which she learns can only be ended when her own life is threatened. In fact, at one point in the novel she is forced to experience slavery firsthand.

Even Dana's observations of life for the plantation's slaves are grim enough, but Butler's use of a first-person narrator makes the novel read like a modern-day slave narrative, reminiscent of the accounts written by former slaves about what they suffered under slavery.[6] This makes the novel often painful to read, but *Kindred* is a stark reminder of what slavery was like in the United States. On the other hand, Butler's novel is no *Uncle Tom's Cabin,* no melodramatic account of slavery designed solely to move readers. Butler accurately shows that different slaves experienced different situations under different masters, and that some experiences were comparatively better or worse. She also portrays a variety of personalities among the slaves held by Rufus's family. Along the way, Dana—who had read a great deal about slavery but who judged it from her limited experience—comes to a greater understanding of how slavery affected the people under it, both slaves and masters.

As part of this, Butler deals with the complicated relationships between slaves and masters, in particular through Rufus and a slave named Alice, both of whom, Dana comes to learn, are her ancestors. Thus Dana, who at times would just as soon let Rufus perish as the "peculiar institution" warps his childhood innocence into an acceptance of slavery's evils, is driven to preserve his life through the grandfather paradox, the classic puzzle of time-travel stories. If she lets Rufus die before he and Alice can conceive the child who would, over time, start the family that eventually leads to Dana, would she cease to exist? Not wanting to find out, she is forced to watch out for Rufus and even to serve as a means of her slave ancestor's sexual exploitation. *Kindred* therefore is not only an ingenious time-travel novel and a fictional though nonetheless disturbing depiction of American slavery but also a thought-provoking exploration of moral choices.

Yet Butler complicates this uneasy situation further by making Dana's husband, Kevin, white. They experience prejudice as an interracial couple in the United States of the 1970s, and when

Kevin travels with her to antebellum Maryland at one point, while holding her as she is "called" by Rufus, to survive they must adopt the roles of master and slave, with the assumption that Kevin also uses her sexually. Additionally, when Kevin is stranded in the past for a number of years (his time) before Dana is called back, she has reason to worry how living in a culture that accepts the secondary status of African Americans as natural has affected him.

Kindred is a stunning achievement, a contemporary novel that also reads like historical fiction, with none of the horrors of history softened for contemporary readers. It is a provoking treatment of slavery's legacy and of race relations, as well as a thoughtful depiction of various kinds of love and hatred. Butler herself has called the novel a work of fantasy, since the means of time travel are never revealed, but this is not much different from other time-travel stories, such as Mark Twain's *A Connecticut Yankee in King Arthur's Court* (1889) or Jack Finney's *Time and Again* (1970). Ultimately, what matters is not so much whether the novel is science fiction or fantasy, but its effectiveness as a work of fiction, and *Kindred* is highly effective—and affecting.

Time is also a central concern of Gregory Benford's *Timescape* (1980), which also deals with the past and the near future and the relationship between the two. It is not surprising that Benford, a professor of physics at the University of California–Irvine, can write about science convincingly, and in fact, *Timescape* has often been praised as one of the best novels about how scientists actually work ever written. What is perhaps more surprising is that Benford also writes convincingly about human emotions and relationships, often in prose that evokes modernist masters such as James Joyce and William Faulkner.

The winner of the Nebula Award for 1980, *Timescape* is generally hailed as Benford's best novel.

It is this combination of hard SF and Benford's insightful glimpses into matters of the heart that lends his work its unique quality, even if his stated aims in this novel seem more modest. In the acknowledgments that preface the book, he writes,

> Many scientific elements in this novel are true. Others are speculative, and thus may well prove false. My aim has been to illuminate some outstanding philosophical difficulties in physics. If the reader emerges with the conviction that time represents a fundamental riddle in modern physics, this book will have served its purpose.[7]

If the sole purpose of writing a book of nearly five hundred pages is to make readers aware of difficulties regarding time in modern physics, however, why go to such lengths, as opposed to writing an article for a scientific periodical of around one-tenth the length or less? And why a novel instead of a scientific treatise? Whatever Benford's purpose for his statement about the book's purpose, there is clearly more to *Timescape* than a discussion of theoretical models of time, regardless of the centrality of this subject to the story. In this way, *Timescape* illustrates what is perhaps the fundamental paradox of the genre. Science fiction often deals with science directly, both "true" science and "speculations," to use Benford's language, and some have believed that one of its purposes is to educate readers about science and encourage them to learn more (which in fact has been true for many readers). Yet in this form of writing, science is wedded to fiction, the search for truth about the physical world to imagined settings, situations, and characters. While this might sound like a formula for disaster, and while the balance between the two has often been uneven in SF, at its best science fiction presents readers with the best of both worlds, informative or thought-provoking ideas along with skillful revelations about what it means to be human.

Timescape deals with two sets of characters, scientists at the University of California campus in La Jolla in the early 1960s and at Cambridge University in the late 1990s. (Obviously, for anyone reading this novel in the twenty-first century, this might make the book seem dated, but this is actually not the case, given what Benford does with the ending.) The world of the late twentieth century is in dire straits, filled with ecological catastrophes and rife with shortages of various types. A physicist working with a theoretical particle called a tachyon, which is speculated to travel faster than light and thus backward in time, attempts to use these particles to send messages into the past, hoping to prevent the current situation. The transmissions are received by the scientists in the early 1960s, and change does indeed occur because of them, but not as anticipated. Instead, alternate universes are created, including one in which John F. Kennedy survives the 1963 assassination attempt that killed him in "our" universe. So catastrophe is averted in one universe but not in another—Benford's resolution of the grandfather paradox.

If all of this sounds abstruse and intellectually interesting but not terribly interesting on an emotional level, the actual experience of reading the novel is quite different. For one thing, Benford captures the personal lives of the characters in both times effectively. While struggling with scientific problems, the characters also confront personal problems: family and friends, lovers and spouses, colleagues and competitors, superiors and underlings, and so on. *Timescape,* for all of its theoretical speculations made real, is in many ways a novel about its characters' personal struggles and accomplishments, all set within richly depicted cultural contexts. While much of the story deals with science, much of it also deals with more human matters.

This is also true of Benford's 1981 story "Exposures." An astronomer tries to make sense of an anomalous set of photographic images, an endeavor that parallels his son's struggle with learning to read. Similarly, the images, sent by aliens and warning of the approach of a black hole, consuming whatever comes within reach of its immense gravity, parallels the cancer that threatens his son's teacher. A believer in science rather than religion, the astronomer wonders about the existence of a higher power even while facing the idea that aliens may be trying to help humanity. Macrocosm and microcosm interconnect in evocative ways, and the exposures here are both photographic and personal.

If Benford's best work represents an effective marriage of idea-based science and character-based literature, the works of two writers with whom he is often compared seem more like throwbacks to older models of science fiction in which ideas are central and characterization secondary. This is not to say that either David Brin or Greg Bear (discussed in chapter 4) does a poor job of creating characters, but rather that they do so less effectively than Benford at his best, with their work being more reminiscent of past SF stories of independent scientists and adventures in outer space. Much of their work, in fact, could even be labeled as "space opera," an old term referring to a type of epic science fiction containing things such as galactic empires and cosmic battles. This and more can be found in Brin's Uplift series, which also includes as a central motif the idea of animals being raised to human levels of intelligence.

The Uplift series begins with Brin's first novel, *Sundiver* (1980). In this novel and others in the series, Brin takes some of the standard SF motifs, such as contact with aliens, space opera, uplifted animals, and the idea of an alien race seeding the stars with life, mixes them together, and manages to make something new rather than unoriginal and derivative. The story begins on twenty-third-century Earth. Humanity has made contact with alien races who are part of a galactic network, billions of years old, in which different races have uplifted others to sentience. Humanity has done the same with chimpanzees and dolphins but stands out as having no "patron" race that has done this for them. There are two factions on Earth: the Shirts (Danikenites), who believe humans were uplifted by an alien race, and the Skins (Neolithics), who believe humanity raised itself through evolution. In the meantime, humans, aided by alien technology, are exploring the sun in manned expeditions to investigate possible answers to these questions.

Like Butler's later Xenogenesis trilogy (discussed in chapter 4), humanity is depicted as self-destructive (also a theme in Benford's *Timescape*) and in need of alien assistance; yet humanity is also able to take care of itself, and as the Uplift series develops, Brin basically returns to the Golden Age notion of humanity's innate superiority, as readers see humanity rising from its humble position among the races of the universe to achieve preeminence. Yet Brin's treatment of human problems and human potential is more nuanced and sophisticated than the naive optimism of much earlier SF.

The same could be said of the treatment of gender in *Sundiver*, although in some ways the book seems somewhat reactionary on this score. Often the third-person omniscient narrator will describe a female character by noting her physical attractiveness, as in the first chapter: "As usual, she was wearing next to nothing. Pretty, well endowed, and with long black hair, the young biologist wore next to nothing very well." To be fair, the novel also comments upon women's intelligence and competence as scientists and leaders, and women here also comment upon the attractiveness of men. Yet other parts of the novel related to gender stand out. Helene deSilva, the "Confederacy Commandant" on Mercury, is described by her male superior as his "right-hand man," and the narrator later says, "Occasionally a man, male or female, would lean forward and peer at some detail on a screen."[8] He does this again in chapter 28 of the next novel in the series, *Startide Rising* (1983; revised 1985).[9] Perhaps these oddities represent a transitional phase in standard English usage, a shift from thinking of "man" as including both men and women (a usage so richly mocked in Joanna Russ's 1975 novel *The Female Man*) to the avoidance of this usage, or perhaps Brin is suggesting that "man" might again revert to its previous usage. But a more reactionary reading is supported by other parts of *Sundiver*, such as this passage: "At the time Jacob thought her grimness was excessive. Though he could understand her feelings, it was a shame to masculinize those lovely features."[10]

If *Sundiver* at times seems rather conservative, a feature shared by much hard SF, at other times it effectively delivers the traditional science fiction sense of wonder, from Brin's adroit depictions of aliens and uplifted chimps and dolphins to his description of what it might be like to pilot a spacecraft into the sun to his descriptions, recalling Joe Haldeman's *Forever War*, of time dilation on space travelers:

> She shook her head. I'm glad this tour is over soon. Maybe things will be better in another fifty years.

She didn't hold out much hope for that. Already the only place where you could hear a Beatles tune performed was by a symphony orchestra, of all the monstrosities. And good jazz didn't exist outside of a library.

Why did I ever leave home?[11]

Better known are the next two books in Brin's Uplift series, *Startide Rising* and *The Uplift War* (1987). Set two hundred years after *Sundiver, Startide Rising* was extremely popular with readers and writers alike, winning both the Hugo and Nebula; *The Uplift War* also received the Hugo. In both novels, the sentient species of Earth—humans, chimps, and dolphins—come into conflict with the galactic Patrons who oversee the uplift of the universe's potentially intelligent species but who cannot account for intelligence emerging on Earth without their guidance and are uncomfortable with both Earth's curiosity and what its species discover. When matters are revealed to be different from what the Patrons had told them, the races of Earth take a stand against those who would suppress them.

It is difficult to imagine a work of fiction in which the American mythos becomes metaphor more forcefully than in Brin's Uplift series. Earth's sentient species, unlike the more staid and cautious older races of the universe, are ambitious, energetic, and lacking in reverence for established ways of doing things. They are like the Americans in Michel-Guillaume-Jean de Crèvecoeur's *Letters from an American Farmer* (1782): a new breed, independent of the ways of the Old World. The common assumption of humanity's superiority found in much American SF of the Golden Age, which Brin revives for a new era in these space operas, could thus be seen as an extension of the American mythos, which in turn echoes biblical beliefs in the idea of a chosen people. But in Brin's Uplift series, humanity (and by extension the species it uplifts) is special not because it is the select object of God's favor or because of its possession of a unique national identity, but because of its unusual combination of toughness and tenderness, of hard-nosed practicality and starry-eyed optimism.

In addition to this aspect of the Uplift series, part of Brin's appeal for fans may come from the ways in which he combines new scientific speculations, clearly explained for non-initiates, with older traditions of science fiction, in particular space opera. Moreover, in the Uplift series he tends to use the techniques of the modern best seller, breaking up a large story into many brief chapters focusing on the different perspectives of a large cast of characters. Brin also employs many of the standard formulas of popular fiction, such as romance, the coming-of-age story, the story of sexual initiation, and of course the action and adventure of the space opera. The result, as Brian W. Aldiss and David Wingrove put it, is that "Brin is immensely readable, without the pejorative that usually implies."[12] Additionally, for SF fans Brin includes a number of inside jokes and SF allusions.

There are also passages in the series, as in much SF, that evince science fiction's second great paradox, besides the strange commingling of (usually) factual science and fictional narrative that drives the genre. In science fiction that depicts the future, authors are forced into the paradoxical situation of describing the future in terms of the present, thus underscoring the story's status as a work of fiction in ways that would delight a deconstructionist critic. For example, consider the following passage from Brin's *Startide Rising*:

The most formal Anglic, spoken carefully by a neo-dolphin, would be difficult for a human raised only in Man-English to understand. The syntax and many root words were the same.

> But a pre-spaceflight Londoner would have found the sounds
> as strange as the voices that spoke them.[13]

Here a perfectly plausible future development, the evolution of English centuries hence into something that a contemporary speaker of English would have difficulty comprehending, is described not in this future version of English or an even later version of the language, which would make sense given that the novel is narrated in the past tense, but in the English of the pre-spaceflight Londoner, thus pointing to the novel's status as a crafted artifact of its own time rather than, despite its presentation as such, a historical chronicle of times past. (Then there are occasionally dated references, such as the allusion to $33\frac{1}{3}$-rpm records in chapter 37.) To be sure, if Brin had attempted to write a novel in an extrapolated future English rather than in the English of the 1980s, his readers would no doubt experience as much difficulty as his hypothetical prespaceflight Londoner, and most SF authors choose the simpler if paradoxical route of describing their future worlds in words rooted in the present of the readers rather than of the characters. On the other hand, SF authors routinely throw in words and phrases that make no sense to contemporary readers but that readers can assume *do* make sense to the characters in the story. Occasionally, authors go to even greater lengths. In the British novel *A Clockwork Orange* (1962), for instance, author Anthony Burgess uses a first-person narrator who speaks an altered English heavily influenced by Russian, while in the postapocalyptic *Riddley Walker* (1980), American expatriate Russell Hoban logically takes linguistic change to its extreme:

> Every 1 knows about Bad Time and what come after. Bad
> Time 1st and bad times after. Not many come thru it a live.

There come a man and a woman and a chyld out of a bern-
ing town they sheltert in the woodlings and foraging the bes
they cud. Starveling wer what they wer doing. Dint have no
weapons nor dint know how to make a snare nor nothing.[14]

Usually, however, science fiction makes demands on its readers
other than at the level of words and sentences.

One of the most important works of American science fiction in the 1980s, which serves as an excellent example of how
an author can combine high literary craftsmanship with accessible storytelling, is Gene Wolfe's four-volume work *The Book of
the New Sun*. Composed of *The Shadow of the Torturer* (1980),
The Claw of the Conciliator (1981), *The Sword of the Lictor*
(1982), and *The Citadel of the Autarch* (1983), *The Book of the
New Sun* is not a tetralogy of related novels but a single novel
published in four books, each devoted to describing a particular
stage in the life of its protagonist, Severian. SF critic John Clute
calls the novel "a profound meditation on history, God, time,
and power" but laments that Wolfe's publisher "gave it dust
jackets that evoke Brak the Barbarian," hardly the first time a
substantial work of SF has been undermined by cover art that
makes it look as if it were just another piece of sci-fi or sword-
and-sorcery hackwork.[15]

For readers knowing enough not to judge a book by its
cover, Wolfe's *Book of the New Sun* offers many of the traditional motifs of science fiction, such as aliens and robots, and in
particular the motifs of future history, such as the dying Earth,
in a radically new fashion that transcends the stylistic experimentation of the New Wave or its self-conscious flouting of old
SF taboos. In form, however, Wolfe's novel is hardly radical, as
the story concerns Severian's life from youth to adulthood,
which he narrates. Stripped to its essentials, the novel details

Severian's upbringing as an orphan, his rebellion against authority and resulting exile, his adventures in the larger world, and his return as ruler of the realm. In its depiction of youth and maturity and in its hero-makes-good narrative, *The Book of the New Sun* resembles many other works of fiction. What is different is the setting within which Severian grows to manhood, the manner in which he narrates his story, and the rich complexity of ideas connecting character to time and place and our world to the world of the novel.

If Jack Vance's novel *The Dying Earth* (1950) is SF's seminal treatment of an earth of the far-distant future, surely Wolfe's novel is the definitive treatment of the concept. As in Vance's novel, the line between technology and magic has become blurred. Earth is now known as Urth, which is imperiled on more than one front: the sun is dying out, the planet's resources are tapped out, and civilization is all but worn out. Wolfe's highly detailed exploration of this setting is one of the most remarkable examples of world building in science fiction or fantasy literature, where setting is often considered on an equal level with characterization or plot, and in fact is sometimes considered as a character in its own right.

Yet *The Book of the New Sun* is indeed a novel in which character and plot are central, and the uncertainties that run through Severian's narrative add to the novel's interpretive richness. In one of the novel's many paradoxes, Severian possesses a flawless memory yet is an unreliable narrator, crafting his story for his own purposes rather than giving an objective account of his life. Nor, despite the first-person narrator, is Severian's the only voice within the work. For instance, recalling Ursula K. Le Guin's samples of alien folklore in *The Left Hand of Darkness* (1969), readers are presented throughout with excerpts of the fables contained in the book Severian keeps with him, *The Book of the Wonders of Urth and Sky,* which add to the texture of the overall work.[16] And of course there are the many characters the protagonist encounters throughout the long novel.

Another of the novel's paradoxes concerns language. Unlike Brin and many other SF writers, who describe things centuries hence as though writing for a contemporary audience (which, of course, they are), Wolfe here employs a distinctive diction for this tale of the far future, but the language seems not so much futuristic as ancient, which contributes to the feeling that the novel is fantasy or perhaps science fantasy despite the solid SF content. Nor is this an echo of the famous opening of *Star Wars:* "A long time ago, in a galaxy far away." The setting is clearly this world, not in the far-flung past but in the distant future. Despite certain parallels, *The Book of the New Sun* is not a fairy tale.

If anything, one is tempted to read the novel as an allegory or a parable. Severian is something of a messiah figure, destined to be autarch from his birth, a worker of miracles and an intermediary between humanity and a higher power (in this case aliens of uncertain intent). Yet he is an ambiguous messiah: the Torturer who also acquires the healing Claw of the Conciliator, one who raises the dead yet also fights in combat. In the novel's sequel, *The Urth of the New Sun* (1987), he functions as a redeemer of the dying Earth, yet his act of salvation results in numerous deaths.

Ultimately, Clute says, "*The Book of the New Sun,* all 400,000 grave and polished words of it, is far greater than the sum of its parts."[17] Indeed, several SF critics and historians have claimed that a simple discussion of the novel's story, setting, or themes insufficiently deals with its status as what many of them proclaim a masterpiece. Its most ardent defender has been Clute, who speaks of the work's greatness being in part due to its "strangeness," echoing the critical pronouncements of mainstream literary critic Harold Bloom. For instance, Clute writes of Wolfe,

> He may be, as a creator of autonomous works of art, the greatest writer of sf in a century which saw many hundreds of writers do their work with high ambition and remarkable craft; he is, however, far from the most important sf writer of the century, and is by no means a writer of great significance in determining the flow of his chosen genre. . . .
>
> A synoptic view of a collective enterprise such as the genre of sf must necessarily deal with those writers whose influence—whether or not we have a high opinion of their œuvres as autonomous works of art—is centrally collegial; and whose own works reflect in turn the influence of others in the long conversation of genre. But synopsis can become travesty when confronted with the essential *strangeness* of the great writer; and any survey of a field or an era . . . fails at the moment it attempts to domesticate that strangeness.
>
> Though Gene Wolfe is not therefore an exemplary figure of the past two decades of sf, he remains an author whose works are so deeply imbricated in the genre that it is absolutely impossible to think of them as transcending genre . . . ; rather than transcending genre, they are genre wrought to the uttermost.[18]

Clute, as much a deliberate stylist as Wolfe, is more to the point at the conclusion of his 1983 review of *The Citadel of the Autarch:* "You must read it."[19]

If, as Clute claims in his entry on Wolfe in *The Encyclopedia of Science Fiction,* Wolfe from the beginning of his career "created texts which—almost uniquely—married Modernism . . . and sf"[20] and thus warrants close reading and scholarly analysis, the career of Philip K. Dick presents readers with another phenomenon entirely: a commercial author who wrote quickly, perhaps too quickly in many cases, yet who has since been acclaimed as one of the geniuses of his field. Dick's work has inspired (for better or worse) more motion-picture adaptations than that of any other American SF author, and his fiction has been the subject of more scholarly attention than that of any other American SF author, with the possible exception of Ursula K. Le Guin. If Wolfe from the start was a conscious craftsman, Dick was an artist whose genius permeates a body of work of rather uneven literary quality.

Dick's most notable work was published in the 1960s, in particular the alternate-history classic *The Man in the High Castle* (1962) as well as *Martian Time-Slip* (1964), *The Three Stigmata of Palmer Eldritch* (1965), and *Do Androids Dream of Electric Sheep?* (1968),[21] although he produced interesting stories and novels from the 1950s to his death in 1982. Although much of his later work is riddled with visionary strains, a late story, "Frozen Journey" (1980), provides a good example of his most characteristic themes, paranoia and the uneasy relation between illusion and reality.

First published in *Playboy,* long interested in publishing science fiction, "Frozen Journey" involves a man on a years-long flight to another planet. The passengers, the only humans on the spaceship, are placed in cryogenic suspension, but something goes wrong with the protagonist's system and he wakes up. As the ship lacks full life-support systems, he cannot be released from his "frozen" state, but the artificial intelligence operating the ship also realizes that he will go insane after only a few days, let alone years, of sensory deprivation. The man and the computer agree that the best course is to allow the computer to induce at first memories and then, when the memories prove traumatic, new experiences within the man's mind. The end result, however, is that even when the trip is finally over, the man has lived through the landing and subsequent experiences so many times in his head, thanks to the computer, that he can no longer distinguish between computer-induced illusion and reality. Thus the well-intended computer becomes something similar to the demon of René Descartes' *Meditations on First Philosophy* (1641), and the man is forced into the Cartesian role, unable to know whether or not he is being deceived, and "Frozen Journey" becomes a short, simple story not only about traditional SF concerns, such as voyages into space and the colonization of other worlds, but also about psychological and philosophical matters.

Similarly, in a story by a writer at the beginning of his career rather than the end, illusion and reality are interestingly compared and confused. While he would later gain fame as one of the founding fathers of a branch of science fiction known as cyberpunk (discussed in chapter 4), William Gibson gained attention with a number of stories published in the late 1970s and early 1980s, among them "The Gernsback Continuum" (1981).[22]

Before considering this particular story, however, the issue of whether Gibson is an fact an American writer should be addressed. Born in 1948 in South Carolina, Gibson has lived in Canada since the late 1960s, and he is included in the volume *Canadian Fantasy and Science-Fiction Writers* in the Dictionary of Literary Biography series.[23] But for that matter, so is Brian Moore, a native of Ireland who immigrated to Canada and became a Canadian citizen yet spent most of his career in California. And where does one place an author such as Geoff Ryman, who was born in Canada, spent part of his youth in the United States, and now resides in England? In the end, of course, what matters is not the ability to connect an author with a particular nationality but whether that author is worth reading. And in the case of Gibson, despite his lengthy residence in Canada, he was certainly a major influence on cyberpunk, which was a significant development in American science fiction. As for "The Gernsback Continuum," the story is a trenchant critique of both the contemporary world and the history of American science fiction.

Hugo Gernsback, as noted in the introduction, was the first to edit a magazine devoted entirely to science fiction, which he is credited with naming, and the Hugo Award given annually at the World Science Fiction Convention is named in his honor. Gernsback saw science fiction as a means of teaching readers about science and of promoting scientific and technological development. In a field that has long classified writers and works as either optimistic or pessimistic, Gernsback was decidedly an optimist, seeing in science the way to a better, brighter future.

In "The Gernsback Continuum," the protagonist is a photographer assigned by a book editor, Dialta Downes, to shoot examples of "'futuristic' Thirties and Forties architecture you pass daily in American cities without noticing: the movie marquees ribbed to radiate some mysterious energy, the dime stores faced with fluted aluminum, the chrome-tube chairs gathering dust in the lobbies of transient hotels" (30). This futuristic yet historical architecture is explicitly connected with science fiction stories, pulp-magazine artwork of the same period, and movies such as *Metropolis* (1926) and *Things to Come* (1936), as the photographer flips through other photos:

> I saw a dozen shots of Frank Lloyd Wright's Johnson's Wax Building, juxtaposed with the covers of old *Amazing Stories* pulps, by an artist named Frank R. Paul; the employees of Johnson's Wax must have felt as though they were walking into one of Paul's spray-paint pulp utopias. Wright's building looked as though it had been designed for people who wore white togas and Lucite sandals. (30)

The first-person narrator's attitude toward these strange artifacts of the past, which he calls "elaborate props for playing at living in the future" (30), is one of ironic detachment, as in the following passage:

> They put Ming the Merciless in charge of designing California gas stations. Favoring the architecture of his native Mongo, he cruised up and down the coast erecting raygun emplacements in white stucco. Lots of them featured superfluous central towers ringed with those strange radiator flanges that were a signature motif of the style, and made them look as though they might generate potent bursts of raw technological enthusiasm, if you could only find the switch that turned them on. (32)

But then, while preparing to photograph "a particularly lavish example of Ming's martial architecture" (32–33), he sees in the sky a silver aircraft like none known in 1980, a boomerang-shaped airplane with twelve engines.

Thus begin his visions of a world that never was, the future of the past that never developed into the present as we know it. These culminate in a desert vision of an enormous futuristic city, the airspace of which is filled with dozens of exotic ships and fly-ers. Two of the city's denizens appear before him:

> They were blond. They were standing beside their car, an alu-minum avocado with a central shark-fin rudder jutting up from its spine and smooth black tires like a child's toy. . . . They were both in white: loose clothing, bare legs, spot-less white sun shoes. . . .
>
> They were the children of Dialta Downes's '80s-that-wasn't; they were Heirs to the Dream. They were white, blond, and they probably had blue eyes. They were Ameri-can. Dialta had said that the Future had come to America first, but had finally passed it by. But not here, in the heart of the Dream. Here, we'd gone on and on, in a dream logic that knew nothing of pollution, the finite bounds of fossil fuel, or foreign wars it was possible to lose. They were smug, happy, and utterly content with themselves and their world. (37)

Rather than finding this vision inspiring, however, the protago-nist is frightened by it, not only because he fears he has lost his sanity but also because of another association he makes. Earlier he had connected art deco futurism with the science fiction of the 1930s and 1940s, but he also connects these architectural styles and artistic visions with Nazi Germany: "When I isolated a few of the factory buildings . . . they came across with a kind of sinister totalitarian dignity, like the stadiums Albert Speer built for Hitler" (31). Similarly, in studying the rather Aryan models of the future United States in his vision, along with their smug confidence as representatives of a race of masters if not indeed a master race, the narrator says, "It had all the sinister fruitiness of Hitler Youth propaganda" (38).

Thus it is not surprising that at the end of the story, trying to clear these visions from his head, he seeks out news stories of energy crises, seeming to take comfort in the fact that his world, for all its problems, at least is not the soulless and somewhat sinister utopia of the science fiction magazines published by Gernsback. His exchange with the newsstand owner is particularly telling. First, he notes that the proprietor is African American, in contrast to the lily-white "futuroids" of his vision. Our world may not be utopia, it is suggested, but at least in its diversity it lacks the racist overtones of Gernsbackian SF. This suggestion is made explicit in his conversation with the newsstand owner. "Hell of a world we live in, huh?" the owner says. "But it could be worse, huh?" To which the narrator replies, "That's right . . . or even worse, it could be perfect" (40).

Things are indeed worse in Octavia E. Butler's 1983 short story "Speech Sounds," a disaster story—a common SF story type. But the disaster here is an uncommon one: a plague has not only killed many people but also affected the survivors' ability to create and comprehend language, resulting in the virtual decline of civilization. While some vestiges of modern civilization remain, humanity is reduced to near-total anarchy, stripped of the language that separates it from the lower animals. In particular, women are at the mercy of predatory males (an echo of Farmer's Riverworld series). Not everyone has been equally affected by the plague, however. For instance, the protagonist of the story, a former history professor, can speak and understand language but not read; the man who rescues her from a mob resentful of her abilities can read but not speak. Both characters try to rescue a woman pursued by a man. In the end, the woman's children, whose language abilities seem unimpaired, are taken in by the protagonist, who lost her own family in the plague. This represents a new hope for her life, as the fluent children represent a new hope for the human race.

Butler's story is both disturbing and hopeful, a reminder of the fragility of civilization and of the barrier between humanity and the brutes as well as a celebration of humanity's nobler impulses, of a nobility of character that is willing to give up something of itself for a higher cause. The story is also a good example of the way in which many works of science fiction operate. Similar to James Tiptree Jr.'s story "The Women Men Don't See," it begins normally enough, on a bus between Los Angeles and Pasadena. Only gradually does Butler reveal that the setting is not contemporary southern California but an altered version of it, transformed by the effects of the plague. In the body of the story, readers realize that speech is rare here, something to be hidden for fear of the consequences, so that by the time readers reach the conclusion, where the protagonist encounters the unaffected children, something that would seem perfectly ordinary in a mainstream story—children speaking—becomes extraordinary. Such shifts, from the world we think we know to a world somewhat different from ours, from something we consider normal to something portrayed as abnormal, are typical of much science fiction.

Yet for all of these effects, the reading of this story and other SF works can be jarring in another way, when particular details reflect the period in which the work was written but are out of place in the future world of the story. In the case of "Speech Sounds," this occurs when the third-person narrator provides some exposition about the plague: "As it swept over the country, people hardly had time to lay blame on the Soviets (though they were falling silent along with the rest of the world)."[24] Although the Soviet Union still existed in 1983, and although this comment would have made sense to readers as applying to the near-future setting of the story prior to the collapse of the Soviet Union, for readers following the fall of the USSR, this comment renders the story less plausible as fiction set in the future and more obviously a product of its own times, more obviously a fictional artifact rather than a realistic depiction of a future possibility.

As one can see from even such a cursory view of American science fiction from the late 1970s to the early 1980s, while there were some similarities, in both content and style, among different works, there also was a great deal of diversity, and no unifying thread that ran throughout the period. As SF editor and anthologist David G. Hartwell notes, in the 1970s and early 1980s, "the field began to lose its coherence through sheer size and diffusion."[25] Some of the factors that contributed to SF's growth and diffusion include the renewed popularity of fantasy and its increasing incorporation into science fiction, along with mergers of science fiction and fantasy found in science fantasy, the development of tie-ins, and simple numerical growth, to the point that it was no longer possible, as it once had been, for anyone to read all the American science fiction books and magazine stories published in any given year.

American science fiction became more diverse in other ways as the 1970s ended and the 1980s began. Hartwell, writing in 1984, called this "a time of consolidation," in which different strands of SF were integrated into new syntheses, such as the combination of New Wave experimentalism and its focus on inner space with hard SF in Pohl's *Gateway*.[26] Some onlookers viewed such developments with horror, feeling that the field had lost its sense of unity and had betrayed its sense of identity by exposing itself to outside influences and attempting to reach a larger audience. Others felt that these developments were precisely what American science fiction needed. Moreover, the field was becoming more diverse in its writers and readers as well. Although men remained in the majority, female authors and readers were entering science fiction in substantially increasing numbers during the 1970s and 1980s, resulting in some changes in the nature of the fiction on the part of both male and female writers. Further, in a field that had long been dominated by white writers (many of them Jewish), a small minority of African American authors, most notably Samuel R. Delany and Octavia E. Butler, increasingly became visible. Finally, reflecting similar developments in the larger culture, openly gay and lesbian writers, most notably Delany and Joanna Russ, entered the field.

The issue of increased diversity, however, was most apparent in the fiction itself. The growth in the number of readers as well as the number of titles published solidified a development that could not have come to pass earlier, namely, the fragmentation of the field. Science fiction had always included different types of stories, and readers had always preferred some types of stories over others, but now it was possible for readers to focus on a specific type of SF—feminist, military, alternate-history, hard, *Star Trek* novels—to the exclusion of others if they so chose, a trend that would only become more pronounced throughout the 1980s and into the 1990s. To be sure, many SF readers still remained catholic in their tastes (at least where SF was concerned, and for some even beyond SF), but for writers this increased diversity was something of a mixed blessing. While more readers meant a larger potential audience, the fragmentation of the field meant that many writers would appeal to only a fraction of that audience. It is little wonder, then, that as the 1980s progressed many SF publishers and writers were on the lookout for something exciting and new, something that would perhaps reunify the field. It did not happen, but something close to it came in that most science fictional of literary years, 1984.

CHAPTER 4

Cyberpunk and Other Trends, 1984–1992

As the year 1984 began, the most-discussed science fiction novel among the general public was British author George Orwell's *Nineteen Eighty-Four,* published in 1949. Much discussion and debate ensued about how accurately Orwell had predicted future events or whether the novel was intended to be taken as a prediction at all. Many comparisons were made between the totalitarian society of the novel and the contemporary society of 1984.

One science fiction story published in 1984, "The Life of Anybody" by Robert Sheckley, provides an interesting commentary on Orwell's dystopian vision as well as a prescient prediction of its own. The premise of this very short story is that, uninvited and unexpected, television crews could descend upon anybody's household at any time to film the everyday goings-on within. The object for both the television producers and their unsuspecting subjects is complete and total realism; if the producers think the people are acting differently from how they would normally act if they were not being watched, the cameras stop rolling. In *Nineteen Eighty-Four,* citizens are monitored constantly by the government by means of "telescreens," an unwelcome invasion of personal privacy, while in Sheckley's story people actually welcome the presence of cameras recording their every move, anxious to experience their fabled fifteen minutes of fame. In this story, to paraphrase Nicole Kidman's character in the movie *To Die For* (1995), you are nobody unless you are on television—a funny and not-so-subtle critique of popular media and people's obsession with fame, as well as an ironic inversion of Orwell's nightmare vision.

This 1984 story also anticipates, in a stunningly accurate fashion, the reality-TV boom of the late 1990s and early 2000s. Again, it was not as if Sheckley predicted the phenomenon wholesale; rather, like many SF writers, he took a look at existing trends—in this instance the popularity of television, including precursors to later reality shows, along with the desire of many people to be famous, even if temporarily—and extrapolated a possible development of these trends. In so doing, he uncannily foresees the reality-TV phenomenon, for which he steadfastly refuses to take the blame.[1]

While much attention was paid to Orwell's best-known book during the year he assigned as its title, by the end of 1984 the most discussed novel in the science fiction field was not Orwell's dystopia but another futuristic dystopian book, written by an erstwhile American living in Canada: William Gibson's *Neuromancer.* This novel created more discussion and debate in American SF than anything since the New Wave of the late 1960s and early 1970s, and no American SF novel was as much the center of attention or as widely imitated as was *Neuromancer.* If in his earlier story "The Gernsback Continuum" Gibson had critiqued pulp-magazine science fiction and contrasted its somewhat totalitarian visions with the rather imperfect world of the present, in *Neuromancer* and its sequels he provides glimpses of a near future that, for all its technological prowess, seems an uninviting place in which to live.

This dark tone is established with the novel's well-known opening sentence, "The sky above the port was the color of television, tuned to a dead channel,"[2] echoing the opening of T. S. Eliot's poem "The Love Song of J. Alfred Prufrock" (1915) with its comparison of the evening sky to a patient etherized upon a table. This is a dark, grimy world, due in part to two of Gibson's influences: the hard-boiled detective fiction of the 1930s and 1940s, especially the work of Raymond Chandler and Dashiell Hammett, and *Blade Runner* (1982), Ridley Scott's cinematic adaptation of Philip K. Dick's *Do Androids Dream of Electric Sheep?* (1968), a literally dark movie that owes a great deal to the film noir movies based on crime fiction of the 1930s and 1940s. The world of Gibson's *Neuromancer* is one of multinational corporations and organized crime in which characters escape the squalor of their lives through drugs and in "cyberspace," a term Gibson coined in his story "Burning Chrome." It denotes a computerized reality as opposed to the three-dimensional world, with which "meat puppets" could interact by "jacking in":

> Cyberspace. A consensual hallucination experienced daily by billions of legitimate operators, in every nation, by children being taught mathematical concepts. . . . A graphic representation of data abstracted from the banks of every computer in the human system. Unthinkable complexity. Lines of light ranged in the nonspace of the mind, clusters and constellations of data. Like city lights, receding . . .[3]

All of this is depicted in a tough, hard-boiled style, reflected through a youth culture that has much in common with the punk phenomenon of the 1970s and 1980s, especially its critiques of political power and social institutions and its uncertainty about offering better alternatives. Hence the name of the

SF movement to which *Neuromancer* was seen as a seminal text, a combination of punk attitude and cybernetics: cyberpunk.

Neuromancer deals with many of the traditional subjects of science fiction, such as global economies, artificial intelligence, urbanization, and social change, and the plot essentially draws upon the conventions of the thriller. What is different, if not exactly new, is Gibson's adroit combination of these traditional SF motifs and modes with emerging revolutions in communications technology. Gibson was one of the first SF authors, and certainly the first to do so in such a popular novel, to explore how computers might communicate with one another via the Internet (here called the matrix) and with human beings. Also, again revealing the influence of *Blade Runner* as well as contemporary business trends, he was one of the first English-language SF authors to consider seriously the possibility of a world economy dominated not by the United States or Europe but by Asia, specifically Japan and China. In fact, much of the culture in the novel, though set largely in North America, has an Asian flavor. But again the street-smart, world-weary tone of hard-boiled detective fiction dominates, as Case, the protagonist of *Neuromancer,* finds himself embroiled in a situation the magnitude of which he is unaware, for all his knowledge of the mean streets. *Neuromancer* and its sequels, *Count Zero* (1986) and *Mona Lisa Overdrive* (1988), collectively constitute the Sprawl trilogy, which expands upon the original story of the first novel to investigate industrial espionage and the development of a form of artificial intelligence.

Gibson never accepted credit for inventing cyberpunk as a name[4] or as a movement, but *Neuromancer* nonetheless became a focus for discussion and debate regarding what many in science fiction saw as the next new thing. The novel influenced a number of first-rate talents and was imitated by a number of lesser writers, and cyberpunk became a major trend within the field. Defenders of the movement—most notably Bruce Sterling, who edited its major collection, *Mirrorshades: A Cyberpunk Anthology,* and whose introduction to that book is perhaps its key manifesto—argued that cyberpunk was the logical development of science fiction in the information age and in the era of urban sprawl and multinational corporations. Those who looked on cyberpunk less favorably claimed that it was yet another manifestation of New Wave pessimism and pretension. American science fiction had long celebrated the belief in basic human decency and in the significance of the knowledgeable, capable individual, but cyberpunk seemed to be saying that humanity was essentially corrupt and that individuals were largely powerless in the face of forces beyond their control. As SF critic John Clute puts it, "This double intuition of *Neuromancer* about the nature of the world to come—that we are hugely empowered, that we are essentially powerless—may be the most profound metaphor constructed by an sf writer for the experience of living in the 1980s and 1990s."[5] In any event, cyberpunk loomed so large on the SF horizon and in the attention paid to it by the mainstream media that it could not be ignored.

Even if cyberpunk seemed to be everywhere in the mid-1980s, other science fiction writers pursued their own agendas and projects, many of which had nothing to do with the field's hot new movement. Two important stories also published in 1984, Octavia E. Butler's "Bloodchild" and "The Lucky Strike" by Kim Stanley Robinson, exemplify this fact.

Butler's "Bloodchild," anticipating her coming Xenogenesis trilogy, deals with sexual relations between humans and aliens in a way that radically challenges traditional notions of gender, here in the story's depiction of a symbiotic relationship between an alien race and the human males they use as hosts of their developing eggs. Moreover, also anticipating the Xenogenesis books as well as looking back at her time-travel novel *Kindred,* questions of sex are inextricably linked to questions of race and of power.

Power is also central to Robinson's "Lucky Strike," although he focuses on issues of military power. The story is an alternate history, a narrative in which something in the past happens differently than we know it did, thereby resulting in an alternate history extrapolated from this change. While alternate history was not new to SF, with notable examples emerging in the 1950s and 1960s, in the 1980s and 1990s American SF experienced an explosion of alternate-history stories and novels.

Robinson's story takes place in the Pacific theater near the end of World War II, as the military prepares to drop atomic bombs on Japanese targets. What first appears to be a historical narrative shifts into alternate history when the crew who in our history participated in the attack on Hiroshima crash during a practice flight. The assignment is then given to another crew, including the bombardier January, who experiences a moral crisis over the thought of being responsible for thousands of civilian deaths and semiconsciously drops the bomb on an unpopulated area instead. Robinson then continues the story to conclude with the peaceful surrender of the Japanese and a worldwide peace movement inspired by January's example, thus offering a revised ending to the conflict.

Robinson's story exemplifies two possible reasons behind the popularity of alternate-history SF, for both readers and writers. The first, which helps to explain why a type of writing that more closely resembles historical fiction than science fiction might nonetheless be considered SF, is that, like other forms of science fiction, it provides a response to the question, What if? More typically in science fiction, this question concerns some matter in the present or usually the future that touches in some way upon scientific or technological factors, or at any rate upon the notion of radical change. For instance, what if, as in Lois McMaster Bujold's *Falling Free* (1988), humans were genetically engineered to have two additional arms instead of two legs in order to be more effective in zero-gravity conditions? Or what if, as in Nancy Kress's *Beggars in Spain* (1993), humans were genetically engineered to live without needing to sleep? Much of the appeal of such stories for SF readers—though not all of it, contrary to the claims of some mainstream critics who believe this is *all* that SF does—lies in seeing how writers develop such ideas, how they extrapolate from an imaginative premise to its possible consequences. In alternate history, the imaginative premise is not something like What if aliens landed on Earth? or What if humans could live for centuries? Rather, it is concepts like What if the Nazis had won World War II? or What if John F. Kennedy had survived the assassination attempt that killed him? From these premises, writers of alternate history extrapolate possible consequences. Thus in Robinson's "Lucky Strike," he explores how the conclusion of the war with Japan in World War II might have been different under different circumstances.

For some critics, this aspect of alternate history is merely a ludic exercise; playing games with history, they argue, might be entertaining, but what is the point? It is not as though history can be changed by imagining how it might have been different, and science fiction should be a literature of possible change, and perhaps even of warning. There is some merit to such criticism when applied to some of the sillier examples of alternate history, especially when authors are tempted to saturate their stories with real historical figures placed in rather unlikely roles, and one does get the sense with much alternate history that its authors are merely saying, "Look at this! Wouldn't it be neat if, say, Gandhi had stayed in England and become prime minister?" One does feel in many of these works that the authors *are* merely playing games with history.

However, regarding the better examples of alternate history, one could defend the form by arguing that alternate history done well serves as a reminder of the contingency of history, the fact that there is no foreordained plan that historical events are meant to fulfill. At its roots, most alternate history, like most science fiction, is a naturalistic form of literature, assuming that we live in a universe that is either godless or in which supernatural powers do not intervene, in which things turn out the way they do simply because of complex though comprehensible forces. Just as the people caught up in historical events do not know at the time how things will ultimately turn out, so there is no reason why things could not have turned out differently if certain factors had been changed. This is not to say the universe in SF is random—far from it—but rather that it is causal, and that different sets of causes could logically produce different sets of effects. Thus Robinson in "The Lucky Strike" is saying in effect that the war with Japan could have ended differently.

He goes further, however, and in so doing touches upon another of the reasons for the existence of alternate-history SF. Although Robinson does not explicitly moralize in the story, it is clear that the author believes that the fictional conclusion of the war with Japan presented in "The Lucky Strike" is an improvement upon actual history. In his story, far fewer people are killed or injured and far less destruction results from January's actions. In noting the contrast between fictional story and actual history, readers can easily see which one is preferable. In this way, Robinson is not only answering the question What if? through imaginative extrapolation but also asking, Why not? He is clearly critiquing the actions of the American military in deciding to drop atomic bombs on large Japanese cities. But why bother to do this nearly four decades after the bombings occurred? It may have been regrettable, it could perhaps have been done differently, but what is the point? The point, perhaps, is that, to refer to philosopher George Santayana's famous statement, those who fail to learn from history are doomed to repeat it. Perhaps Robinson's intent is to make readers think about possible alternatives when confronted with similar decisions in the future. Just as science fiction set in the future is often about the author's present, so might some examples of alternate history set in the past also concern matters in the present or the foreseeable future.

History is also used in a science fiction format in much of the fiction of Connie Willis, who began publishing stories in the 1970s and emerged in the 1980s as one of the major talents in American science fiction and fantasy. Her first collection, *Fire Watch* (1985), gathers her earliest stories, which range from screwball comedy ("Blued Moon") and touching stories of aliens visiting Earth and religious orangutans ("And Come from Miles Around" and "Samaritan," respectively) to postapocalyptic survival ("A Letter from the Clearys") and a disturbing story of incest, rape, and bestiality ("All My Darling Daughters"). It also says something about the traditionalism of much American SF, even after the conscious taboo breaking of the New Wave, that the latter story, unlike the others in *Fire Watch,* was first published in the collection rather than first appearing in one of the science fiction or fantasy magazines—"because," as John Clute claims, "its language and theme were still unacceptable in the US magazine market of 1980."[6]

More traditional is the title story of Willis's collection, the first of a number of stories in which history students from a future England travel to the past to study their subjects firsthand. In "Fire Watch," the subject is St Paul's Cathedral during World War II, specifically during the blitz. Characteristically her time travelers find that, for all of their supposed superiority given their knowledge of history, they are often unable to deal with the circumstances that confront them in the past, much like Butler's protagonist in *Kindred.* Thus the events of Willis's time-travel stories, though set in the past, are still uncertain. Other time-travel works by Willis based on the premise of scholars studying the past by traveling to it include *Doomsday Book* (1992), set largely in the fourteenth century, and the forthcoming *All Clear,* again about the London blitz. In addition, one of Willis's comic novels, *To Say Nothing of the Dog* (1997), also concerns time travel, and her futuristic *Remake* (1994) deals with how technology might transform old movies. Also, two of her novels, *Lincoln's Dreams* (1988) and *Passage* (2001), involve characters who make contact with the past within their heads: a woman experiences Robert E. Lee's dreams in *Lincoln's Dreams,* and in *Passages* another woman has unexplainable memories of the *Titanic* disaster. It would be incorrect to say that Willis is a historical writer who explores history through science fiction, as much of her fiction is set in the future, but much of her work offers an examination of historical issues in a way different from alternate history.

An example of Willis working in a more traditional science fiction mode can be found in her contribution to the shared-world novel *Berserker Base* (1985), which also serves as a representative example of the form. While authors have written about others' literary creations for centuries, particularly in the retelling and revision of myths, the concept of shared-world fiction is very much a product of the age of copyright. Shared-world science fiction may be either a collection of stories by different authors edited by someone who creates the framework for the stories or stories by different authors written in the fictional universe established earlier by an author. Such is the case with *Berserker Base*, which contributes to the Berserker series begun by Fred Saberhagen. In Saberhagen's Berserker novels, humans and other sentient life forms fight for survival against self-replicating machines intent upon destroying all life in the universe. *Berserker Base* is also ostensibly a novel, but it is actually a collection of "braided" stories, to use Clute's term, linked together by an overarching framework. The framework, about a human space pilot captured by the Berserkers and forced to team with an alien so that their combined mentalities can search the galaxy for news of the Berserkers' conflicts against living beings, is provided by Saberhagen. The individual novellas are the separate conflicts they detect, written by a variety of authors: Willis, Stephen R. Donaldson, Roger Zelazny, Poul Anderson, Edward Bryant, and Larry Niven. As one might expect, the result does not read like a novel at all, and the stories are uneven in quality, all of them competent but none of them achieving greatness. They are also, by the end, somewhat predictable: the living beings, tested by the Berserker threat, discover a way to defeat the machines (thus each is a common SF story type, the problem story), and each is, interestingly enough, a love story, generally along the lines of many such stories. A man and a woman get to know each other, they are attracted to each other, some conflict produces a tension in their relationship, and this tension is resolved at the end. All of this is rather formulaic, although handled by able talents, and in addition to serving as an example of shared-world fiction and of the common SF theme of machines as both blessings and threats, *Berserker Base* represents the formulaic nature of much of the material published in the field.

Also somewhat formulaic is George R. R. Martin's *Nightflyers* (1985), which nonetheless provides an interesting example of a writer playing with the formulas. The title story of the collection (1980), like Harlan Ellison's "I Have No Mouth, and I Must Scream" (1967), like the Stanley Kubrick film *2001: A Space Odyssey* (1968), and like Saberhagen's Berserker series, concerns artificial intelligence that develops into a threat. Yet Martin takes this common SF motif into some unusual directions. Like many such stories, "Nightflyers" reads like a horror story, evoking the often-repeated claims that as a genre science fiction has its roots in Gothic fiction, in which characters are confronted with strange, threatening forces. Unlike much Gothic fiction, however, the forces in such SF stories are not supernatural but explicable in terms of the scientific worldview. Yet in "Nightflyers," Martin succeeds in retaining this sense of supernatural dread by having his sentient shipboard computer develop psionic powers.

Martin's story was published five years before being reprinted in this collection, and it anticipates one of the most significant American SF novels of the 1980s, Greg Bear's *Blood Music* (1985), in both motif and mood. The setting of Bear's novel is the near future, a recognizable world of research institutes and the minutiae of contemporary American life. The research that takes the novel into the territory of science fiction is biological, specifically, the attempt to create intelligent cells, which eventually become aware of their hosts' thoughts. Initially the book reads like a horror story; ultimately, it reads like a work of mysticism.

Blood Music, in fact, is filled with shifts and transformations of various types. To begin with, it defies traditional beliefs about character in the modern novel. The book begins with Virgil Ulum, a researcher at a California laboratory, pursuing his own independent studies of the possibility of intelligent cells. The first section of the novel focuses on Virgil, and since this is not a multiple-viewpoint novel such as, say, David Brin's *Uplift War* or Michael Crichton's *Jurassic Park* (1990), readers might reasonably suppose that Virgil is the main character, that the novel will relate the matters of the narrative through his perspective. And this is true, up to a point. Called on the carpet for pursuing his own research with laboratory resources and fearful that his work will be destroyed, he injects his prototype cells into his bloodstream and is soon transformed as the cells rebuild him into something different. Early in the novel, which most readers have been reading with the expectation that Virgil will remain the protagonist throughout, he appears to have been killed, and the story shifts to other characters, becoming more like the multiple-viewpoint model. Thus Bear frustrates the expectations of readers accustomed to being introduced to a central character and following the story through the viewpoint of that particular character. This ties in with one of the central themes of the novel, the idea of transcending the individual personality and joining with other personalities in a group consciousness—a theme in Martin's story "A Song for Lya" (1974) as well—but it also relates to a fact about much science fiction that some mainstream critics see as one of its chief weaknesses but that many who appreciate science fiction cite as one of its strengths: unlike the modern naturalistic novel, for the most part the SF novel is not primarily focused on character but on larger matters, such as the impact of change or of ideas on a whole society. The character shift that Bear presents in *Blood Music* may seem jarring to some readers, but it is appropriate given his subject, which is nothing less than the transformation of the human race.

Other shifts occur in the novel as well. At first, Virgil is elated with what the intelligent cells, which he terms "noocytes," do for him, making him healthier, improving his sex life, and so on. But it gradually dawns on him that the noocytes have an agenda of their own, and in fact he claims to communicate with them. He does not seemed alarmed at what is happening to him, but from the outside the transformation is alarming indeed—and more so with Virgil's girlfriend, whom his friend finds melting into the shower drain. At this point in the story, readers' response will undoubtedly be one of horror. Bear clearly evokes narratives from earlier SF, such as *The Body Snatchers* (1955) by Jack Finney—perhaps better known to the general public in its film incarnations, especially the first two, filmed as *Invasion of the Body Snatchers* (1956, 1978)—and, again from SF cinema, *The Blob* (1958). Both previous narratives involve alien creatures that absorb human beings, which is what the noocytes seem to do as *Blood Music* progresses. The sense of horror is heightened when they escape the confines of Virgil's apartment and head out into the larger world. The story then shifts, as most SF readers would expect, to a disaster story, with humanity threatened by an intelligent plague.

Yet Bear does not leave matters thus, instead offering further shifts in the story. As the narrative expands to encompass a number of viewpoint characters, gradually these characters (and the readers) come to realize that, while it appears that the humans transformed by the noocytes deliquesce into puddles of noocyte-controlled goo, they do not actually die. Instead, their minds are copied by the cells and become part of an increasingly large biological complex, a superbeing that includes the mind of every human who has every been transformed by the noocytes. Ultimately, humanity is transformed and transcends its human limitations to become something greater than it was before. Thus what initially seems like a novel focused on one character comes to encompass all of humanity; what initially seems like horror takes on an almost religious quality.

Readers' responses to all this, of course, will differ. Some, for instance, find Bear's presentation of transcendence intellectually and perhaps even spiritually thrilling, comparing it to other SF narratives of transcendence, such as *2001: A Space Odyssey*, Arthur C. Clarke's *Childhood's End* (1953), or the science fiction of Olaf Stapledon. Others, despite the novel's shift from horror to a scientific explication that presents the noocytes as benign rather than monstrous, nonetheless respond with revulsion or reject the novel's presentation of what is essentially a heaven achieved without death, of godhood attained in a world without God. The more common response among SF readers is that Bear's *Blood Music* is one of the masterpieces of the field, which says as much about the SF community as it does about the book.

Biology is also central to Kurt Vonnegut Jr.'s *Galápagos* (1985), but before considering the novel as a work of contemporary American science fiction it is worth looking at Vonnegut's relation to the field. Vonnegut's earliest works are obviously almost entirely science fiction: *Player Piano* (1952), his first novel, is a dystopian depiction of a society governed by machines; his second, *The Sirens of Titan* (1959), concerns humanity's manipulation by an alien race. Vonnegut's fourth novel, *Cat's Cradle* (1963), centers around a substance created by a scientist that is capable of freezing the world's water, and his fifth, *God Bless You, Mr. Rosewater* (1965), while not SF, includes one of the most quoted passages *about* science fiction ever written, as spoken by the novel's drunken protagonist, who stumbles into a convention of SF writers:

> "I love you sons of bitches," Eliot said in Milford. "You're all I read anymore. You're the only ones who'll talk about the *really* terrific changes going on, the only ones crazy enough to know that life is a space voyage, and not a short one, either, but one that'll last for billions of years. You're the only ones with guts enough to *really* care about the future, who *really* notice what machines do to us, what wars do to us, what cities do to us, what big, simple ideas do to us, what tremendous misunderstandings, mistakes, accidents and catastrophes do to us. You're the only ones zany enough to agonize over time and distances without limit, over mysteries that will never die, over the fact that we are right now determining whether the space voyage for the next billion years or so is going to be Heaven or Hell."[7]

The novel's protagonist later, says the narrator, admitted that "science-fiction writers couldn't write for sour apples, but he declared that it didn't matter":

He said they were poets just the same, since they were more sensitive to important changes than anybody who was writing well. "The hell with the talented sparrowfarts who write delicately of one small piece of one mere lifetime, when the issues are galaxies, eons, and trillions of souls yet to be born."[8]

Thus Vonnegut's fictional creation, presented in a novel that ironically writes humorously if not exactly delicately of one small piece of one mere lifetime, handily recapitulates a debate between science fiction and the mainstream that has raged for decades and that in some ways echoes the controversy between Henry James and his erstwhile protégé H. G. Wells, who later ridiculed his former mentor's obsession with the details of individual lives and argued instead for fiction's engagement with larger issues.[9]

These quotations from God Bless You, Mr. Rosewater, along with his creation of science fiction writer Kilgore Trout, a recurring character in his fiction, parallel Vonnegut's own ambivalence about science fiction.[10] In his early career, Vonnegut clearly saw SF as a means of critiquing society and science, and the science fiction magazines were the first markets that would publish his work. However, he also feared being stuck in the SF ghetto and knew all too well that the general critical disdain for the form could prevent him from achieving wider recognition.

As it turned out, his sixth novel, Slaughterhouse-Five (1969), vaulted him not only to wider recognition but also to the status of a literary superstar, despite its inclusion of science fiction elements in a narrative that drew heavily upon Vonnegut's experiences in World War II. While continuing occasionally to draw upon SF motifs, he would never again be labeled as a science fiction writer; and when confronted with the fact that much of his work did indeed seem to be science fiction, critics who wanted to think of Vonnegut as a literary figure tended to resort to the old mantra "If it's good, it can't be SF"—as if SF, by its very nature, precluded the possibility of quality.

In any event, Vonnegut's late novel *Galápagos* is clearly science fiction, with a touch of the supernatural. The novel is narrated by the ghost of Kilgore Trout's son, who tells how humanity, escaping a worldwide plague, retreats to the Galápagos Islands, an ironic setting given its association with the evolutionary theories of Charles Darwin, and there evolve over the course of millennia into something entirely alien. Like most of Vonnegut's work, the novel is both humorous and sad in its depiction of human foibles.

A postcatastrophe future also provides the setting of David Brin's book *The Postman* (1985), which inspired a partial film adaptation starring Kevin Costner. Although the situation of the novel is grim, with a ravaged humanity scattered into isolated communities and clinging to survival, as in Brin's Uplift novels the book ultimately celebrates the human capacity for endurance and even hope. Similar to Butler's "Speech Sounds," in which one man assumes an outdated role of authority in the face of social chaos, here a drifter dons the uniform of a postal worker and acts as if he represents a government that no longer exists, conveying messages between communities along with the hope that society can rebuild itself. Thus the double meaning of the title: has humanity succeeded it destroying itself, becoming "post-men," or can the human race endure? Brin seems to suggest that it can. While *The Postman* appears to parallel the apocalyptic fears of novels such as Vonnegut's *Galápagos,* in the end it opposes Vonnegut's rueful pessimism with a sense of optimism more characteristic of Brin's work. Interestingly, charges that Brin in *The Postman* was hopelessly naive or romantic came not so much from critics outside the field as from those within it, perhaps revealing that the internal debates between pessimistic and optimistic views in science fiction had not yet subsided, or that Brin had insufficiently made his case in the novel.

Elements of both optimism and pessimism can be seen in Ursula K. Le Guin's science fiction stories set on the West Coast. Earlier works in this setting, such as *The Lathe of Heaven* (1971) and especially "The New Atlantis" (1975), tended toward the pessimistic, both of them utopian in theme and showing how societies that strive for perfection can easily become stifling or totalitarian. In both, capitalistic industrialized cultures are shown as self-destructive. In contrast, the experimental *Always Coming Home* (1985) is, like her earlier novel *The Dispossessed* (1974), an ambiguous utopia, a meditation on the possibilities of a dynamic utopia that rejects the traditionally static utopian visions of the past. While in earlier works such as *The Left Hand of Darkness* (1969) Le Guin had inserted myths and legends into the main narrative, here she employs a plethora of literary styles in an assemblage of fragments that unite to form a picture of a future society in California, ranging from fictional forms to poetry, song, and drama to prose commentary on the various writings. The first edition even included a cassette tape of music by Todd Barton. *Always Coming Home* is thus one of Le Guin's most intriguing and most challenging works in an oeuvre filled with intriguing and challenging works.

Like Brin's *Postman,* Le Guin's *Always Coming Home* concerns the reconstruction of culture following catastrophe, and both novels—and many more SF works of the 1980s besides, both in print and on the screen—reflect contemporary concerns about the possibility of humanity's self-destruction. Yet Le Guin's book is more than a mere cautionary tale, embodying as it does a critique not only of humanity's penchant for destruction through warfare but also its social and ecological sins. Echoing both the pastoral dreams of Brin's *Postman* and the valorization of her pastoral aliens in her earlier *The Word for World Is Forest,* Le Guin presents her matriarchal utopian survivors as working in harmony with the natural world rather than exploiting it. Such utopian imaginings might seem naive, but the postmodern self-reflexivity Le Guin employs here serves as a means of commenting upon and critiquing her own fictional creation.[11]

Although not ostensibly utopian, Norman Spinrad's *Child of Fortune* echoes Delany's *Triton* in its exploration of a future in which humanity has colonized other moons and planets and has found ways to meet humanity's basic needs, leaving people free to explore their own personal agendas in what is essentially a libertarian society. Set in the same fictional and linguistic universe as his earlier *The Void Captain's Tale* (1983), *Child of Fortune* is in many ways a coming-of-age novel, but one considerably different from its mainstream counterparts due to the book's SF content. For one thing, the characters in these novels by Spinrad, as in Delany's *Triton,* enjoy a level of sexual freedom that most readers would consider scandalous in novels with contemporary settings. In both, it is commonly accepted that even teenagers will have multiple sexual partners. What would be labeled promiscuity in narratives with contemporary or historical settings is instead normal in these science fiction worlds. Second, Spinrad presents his readers with a variety of cultures, none presented as superior to another. Again as in Delany, it is taken for granted that people are given the freedom to pursue their own interests, resulting in a plethora of lifestyles existing side by side.

If Delany's protagonist in *Triton* has difficulty coming to terms with who he/she is in a society in which he/she could be practically anything, Spinrad's young protagonist seems surer of herself though still in search of what she wants to do with her life. Thus she embarks upon a tour of the civilized planets, delightedly sampling what they have to offer and taking one lover after another along the way. This "child of fortune" tells her own story, conveyed in a futuristic fusion of English with words from a variety of other languages, and her story culminates in a traditional enough manner: she risks her life to save someone she loves.

Simple description of the novel's plot, characterization, themes, and style, however, does not do justice to the experience of reading *Child of Fortune*. According to some theorists, reading SF brings about a "sense of wonder," which could be as grand as a feeling of transcendence or conceptual breakthrough or as simple as the reaction, "Wow! That's *neat!*" Part of this sense is connected to the experience of reading Spinrad's novel, which seems both familiar and strange. The protagonist's youthful enthusiasm contributes something to this, but the sheer exoticism of the novel, both in setting and in style, are factors as well. In many ways, then, *Child of Fortune* could be called a quintessential science fiction novel, a test case for new readers to determine whether or not they "get it."

Not all SF is so exotic, however. Many works are set closer to the here and now. *Freedom Beach* (1985), for example, a novel by James Patrick Kelly and John Kessel, expanded from one of Kelly's short stories and thus an example of a fix-up novel, is for the most part set in a near future that differs little from the contemporary world. The science fiction departure comes in the form of technology that allows individuals to explore painful experiences in their past and to reach a kind of emotional healing—similar to Karen Joy Fowler's 1985 story "The Lake Was Full of Artificial Things." The novel's many dreamlike scenes allow the authors to tell a variety of stories, some of them humorous despite the serious tone of the book as a whole. For example, at one point a character encounters a robotic Aristophanes who literally brings his comedies to life; at another, the Faust legend is retold as if it were a Marx Brothers movie.[12]

In addition to its SF content, *Freedom Beach* is an example of two trends common in contemporary American science fiction: collaboration and the fix-up. Perhaps more than in any other form of fiction, science fiction abounds in examples of writers working together on an individual work—not only in shared-world books like *Berserker Base* or in novels in which a successful senior author works with a junior partner in developing a concept (a common phenomenon in recent SF), but also in stories and even novels in which the result is intended to be (and often is) a unified narrative composed by equals. Notable examples of SF collaborations include Frederik Pohl and C. M. Kornbluth's novel *The Space Merchants* (1953), the many stories and novels written jointly from the 1940s to the 1970s by the husband-and-wife team of Henry Kuttner and C. L. Moore, and William Gibson and Bruce Sterling's alternate-history novel *The Difference Engine* (1990), in which the invention of a computer in early Victorian England results in a radically changed culture. The fact that SF has traditionally focused on ideas and plot rather than on character and style may be the best explanation for why SF writers are more likely than other authors to work in tandem. Further, as Pohl has said in his presentations and interviews at Science Fiction Research Association conferences, in their early careers he and many of his peers found that collaboration allowed them to compensate for their weaknesses as inexperienced writers and to publish material faster than one person could.[13]

Economics is perhaps the best explanation for the fix-up. Science fiction is one of the few remaining fields of fiction in which most authors get their start writing for the magazines, and these are commercial magazines that pay to publish stories, as opposed to the magazines publishing literary fiction that often pay contributors in copies. Also, while the science fiction magazines require submissions to be of professional quality for publication, they are open to new talent, as opposed to the few paying mainstream markets such as the *New Yorker* or *Playboy*. Thus it is not uncommon for many aspiring SF writers to attempt to place their first efforts with American magazines such as *Analog, Isaac Asimov's Science Fiction Magazine,* and the *Magazine of Fantasy and Science Fiction,* even if these first efforts are parts of planned novels. It is also not uncommon for experienced and successful writers to first publish parts of novels in progress as magazine stories, again for economic reasons: if you can be paid for part of a novel in progress, why not? On the other hand, no one ever became rich writing solely for the magazines, and although book publication was slow to come to the science fiction field, when it arrived it was readily embraced, both for collections of stories published first in magazines— which is how some writers, most notably Harlan Ellison, have done most of their work, even to the present time—and, more and more commonly, for the publication of novels, often novels developed or "fixed up" from magazine stories.

One of the most successful examples of the fix-up is Orson Scott Card's *Ender's Game* (1985). Card's first published story, in fact, was "Ender's Game," which appeared in *Analog* in 1977 and was nominated for the Hugo Award; the following year he received the John W. Campbell Award, given by the fans of the World Science Fiction Convention for the year's best new writer. Card then expanded the story considerably into a novel that was even more successful, launching a popular series and winning both the Hugo and the Nebula. The novel was at once very traditional and highly original, shaped as it was by Card's Mormon faith.

The story revolves around Ender Wiggin, a boy who is part of a eugenics experiment designed by a government fearful of the alien Buggers and hopeful that Ender and other enhanced children will be capable of vanquishing their foe. In the military academy to which he is sent, Ender engages in a series of computerized war games in what at first appears to be practice sessions but what actually are a method for the enhanced Ender to guide real forces in their slaughter of their alien enemies. In many respects, therefore, *Ender's Game* employs many of the classic motifs of traditional SF: the coming-of-age story, the galactic battles of space opera and of military SF, paranoia about the motives of the government and/or the military, and, once the truth is revealed, the notion of the "secret master," the idea of the superior individual whose talents are revealed over the course of the story. Yet in some ways Card takes these traditional materials in a new direction. Rather than depicting the Buggers as the terrifying bug-eyed monsters of the pulp era, it is revealed that they had planned to end the war once they learned that humans were an intelligent species (which also echoes the misunderstanding that launches the conflict in Haldeman's *Forever War*); and rather than depicting humans heroically defending themselves against an alien menace, it is humanity that is guilty of genocide, using a boy as their instrument of destruction. Card thus raises a number of fascinating moral issues, which he pursues in subsequent volumes of the series, particularly in the sequel to *Ender's Game, Speaker for the Dead* (1986). Here the extension of the original novel in a series, while it has profited Card, is more than an effort to milk a successful novel by producing more of the same; instead, it is an effort to continue to explore serious issues unresolved in the first book.[14]

Besides the series' infusion of traditional science fiction approaches with serious moral inquiry and its existence *as* a popular series (Card is one of the few American SF authors to achieve best-seller status), the Ender books are also noteworthy for how Card and his publishers have attempted to cross over to the young-adult market. The later books in the series, which are set in the same fictional universe but feature a different young character, have been aimed primarily at adolescent readers, and *Ender's Game* has been remarketed as a young-adult book. Interestingly, in a field that outsiders often consider adolescent, the emergence of science fiction written or marketed specifically for teenagers is a relatively recent phenomenon, apart from some earlier exceptions such as Robert A. Heinlein's "juveniles." Typically, in the past when teens wanted to read science fiction, they read what was published for an adult readership, and it remains to be seen whether young-adult science fiction will ever attain the success of young-adult fantasy or whether it will, like its adult counterpart, remain a marginal part of the literary landscape, with authors and titles occasionally reaching a larger audience.[15]

The existence of young-adult science fiction, however, is more than an effort to expand the market for SF, although no doubt many publishers are hopeful that SF for younger readers will be as popular as fantasy. First, adolescent literature itself is relatively young, so it is not surprising that little young-adult SF exists. Second, some writers have discovered a talent for writing SF for older children; Nancy Farmer is noteworthy in this respect. But there is also growing concern among many in the science fiction field that the children who in earlier decades would have been drawn to written science fiction are instead being lured to science fiction on television and at the movies, perhaps never to discover SF stories and novels. As a means of addressing a shrinking SF readership, some feel an effort should be made to draw them to written science fiction by writing science fiction specifically for them. Thus Card, in gearing his Ender series toward young adults, may be contributing not only to his own future readership but also to that of SF as a whole.

If Card's depiction of genocide occurs within the context of a story about a young protagonist, Octavia E. Butler's take on the subject is decidedly adult, as well as thematically consistent with much of her other work. Like her earlier story "Bloodchild," Butler's Xenogenesis trilogy—consisting of *Dawn* (1987), *Adulthood Rites* (1987), and *Imago* (1989)—concerns interactions between humans and aliens in which the aliens possess the power and in which sexual relations come into play. But the story touches on other issues as well. Humanity, depicted as inherently self-destructive and thus at an evolutionary dead end, is all but wiped out; only a few have been saved by an alien race known as the Oankali. While SF as it has matured has become increasingly successful at presenting visions of alien life that are truly alien—as opposed to monsters from outer space or beings that are essentially human but with, say, antennae and green skin—Butler's depiction of the Oankali is one of the best treatments of just how alien an alien might be. For one thing, the Oankali possess three genders instead of two, and all three are needed for mating; for another, the Oankali survive through a program of genetic borrowing and adaptation, and their interest in preserving humanity is not so much a matter of altruism as of necessity—they are compelled to interact with other species in a sort of genetic trade. Having saved a segment of humanity from itself, the Oankali then set the terms for humanity's future survival: they plan to adapt themselves using human genetic material, but the humans who wish to breed must allow themselves to be adapted as well by the Oankali. The story focuses on one woman, her lovers, and her friends and family as they face this decision: extinction or radical alteration. Along the way, the Xenogenesis trilogy addresses some of the issues for which science fiction seems most appropriate, particularly the question, What does it mean to be human? Through her story and her characters, both human and alien, Butler shows her readers (as does SF in general) that change is the only constant.

In addition, like Butler's *Kindred*, the trilogy (and especially the first volume, *Dawn*) is interesting in that it features people other than those of European descent as central to the stories being told; and as in "Bloodchild," Butler complicates her SF narratives by challenging, through her human-alien interactions, conventional notions of race. What does "race" mean, after all, in a world in which humans have sexual relations and even children with alien partners? Similarly, she challenges conventional notions of gender, not just in her strong female protagonist in

Dawn but also in her depiction of the Oankali family, in which the female is the largest and most powerful partner.

Although Lois McMaster Bujold's *Falling Free* (1988) is more traditional than Butler's Xenogenesis books, it too concerns questions of genetic alteration and what it means to be human. An engineer is assigned to a mission in space that puts him in contact with a group of young people who have been genetically engineered to work in the weightless conditions of space. To be specific, they possess a second set of arms where their legs normally would be. But while the initial concept is shocking, this is no Frankensteinian horror story involving science turning helpless victims into monsters; rather, the story suggests that such an altered physiognomy makes perfect sense given its context, and the true monsters are those who would use these young people for less-than-noble purposes. At this point, the story becomes a traditional good-versus-evil tale, with the unaltered engineer trying to help these transformed youth from those who would exploit them. It is also a love story, as he falls for one of them—a predictable enough development in many such stories, but given a somewhat unusual twist considering their physical differences. Yet another test for potential SF readers: by the end of the book, are they cheering for the couple to get together or do they respond with revulsion?

Like Butler's Xenogenesis trilogy and Bujold's *Falling Free,* Mike Resnick's stories set in Kirinyaga, a space station that has been crafted to resemble the ecosystem of Kenya by traditionalists who wish to preserve their ancient culture from the onslaught of modern Western values, also challenge readers' beliefs. In "Kirinyaga" (1988), for example, the spiritual leader of the displaced Kikuyu people on this artificial habitat is confronted by a representative of the habitats' administration.

Though he is American educated and possesses a computer, he defends traditional practices, such as leaving the elderly exposed to the hyenas or killing a baby believed to be possessed by a demon, as being right for their people. This and other stories in this setting thus become a test of the extent to which readers are willing to extend the concept of cultural relativism, along with a look at what might be lost or gained as traditional values are obliterated by modern society.

More traditional, though nonetheless compelling, is Geoffrey A. Landis's "Ripples in the Dirac Sea" (1988), which received the 1989 Nebula Award for best short story. It is a time-travel story, but three things distinguish it from more conventional examples of the form. One is the rigor with which Landis fictionalizes the quantum physics that is used to explain the way time travel works in the story—not surprising, since Landis works as a scientist for NASA. The second is the realism with which the difficulties a time traveler might experience in what is effectively an alien environment are presented. Finally, this is a poignant story about memory, loss, and death, one that remains with readers long after they have completed it. Like Resnick's "Kirinyaga" and Bujold's *Falling Free,* Landis's "Ripples in the Dirac Sea" could serve as a test of a potential SF reader. Is he or she capable of enjoying not only the human side of the story but also the scientific premise that underlies it?

If certain SF texts are tests of whether or not readers will appreciate what science fiction has to offer, Dan Simmons's *Hyperion Cantos,* a novel published in two volumes as *Hyperion* (1989) and *The Fall of Hyperion* (1990), provides a complex sampler of almost every conceivable science fiction idea and story type available. Some of these ideas were very much in the air in the mid-to-late 1980s, such as the idea of artificial intelligences running things—also found in Gibson's *Neuromancer* and Card's *Xenocide*. Other ideas draw upon longstanding SF tropes, such as space opera, time travel, entropy, and ecological issues. It is also highly literary in intent, echoing not only the poetry of John Keats, whose long poems *Hyperion* and *The Fall of Hyperion* are about the decline of old gods and the rise of new ones, but also Geoffrey Chaucer's *Canterbury Tales* (late fourteenth century), with the plot of *Hyperion* recounting a pilgrimage to the eponymous planet made by seven travelers who pass the time telling stories. Each of the stories told draws upon a different type of science fiction narrative.

The narrative that unites these disparate strands concerns the planet Hyperion, where the travelers seek the enigmatic Shrike, guardian of the Time Tombs and ambiguous savior. In this sense, as critics have pointed out, the narrative also echoes L. Frank Baum's *The Wonderful Wizard of Oz* (1900), with its quest for a figure who can provide the seekers with something they desire. What the pilgrims desire is redemption, and religious overtones run throughout both *Hyperion Cantos* and its sequels, *Endymion* (1996) and *The Rise of Endymion* (1997), in which the Technocore to which the humans of the Hegemony have pledged their souls allies itself with the Catholic Church. If science fiction, as is often claimed, is a literature of ideas, Simmons provides considerable reflection upon a number of them in these novels, not just concerning religion, but also politics, technology, and psychology. The sheer abundance of these books may overwhelm readers, but Simmons's Hyperion and Endymion novels are among American SF's key achievements of the late 1980s and the 1990s.

Although he had written *Freedom Beach* with James Patrick Kelly in the mid-1980s, another major talent to emerge in the late 1980s and early 1990s was John Kessel, to whom one could direct both critics who look down upon SF and supporters of SF who, despite good evidence to the contrary, persist in believing that science fiction and traditional literary values are ineluctably divorced from each other.

Such an attitude has a lengthy history, of course. It can be traced at least as far back as the split between realist and romantic modes of fiction in the mid-to-late nineteenth century, during which the predecessors of modern science fiction drew heavily from the romantic mode. This history also includes the disdain of many if not all modernist writers and critics for popular culture, within which most American science fiction of the early twentieth century appeared and which has contributed to the widespread academic dismissal of science fiction as subliterary. More recently, the roots of this antiliterary attitude in relation to science fiction include the internal divisions within the genre itself caused in part by the gradual inclusion of science fiction in college and university courses as well as the controversies over the self-consciously literary New Wave of the late 1960s and early 1970s.

Since that time, the already-diverse field of science fiction has fragmented even further, so that a wide variety of styles exist side by side, including a decidedly "literary" type of science fiction, which draws more or less equally from both science fiction traditions and the mainstream heritage. Kessel's science fiction is an excellent example.

It is obvious from Kessel's fiction that he is extremely well read, as his work incorporates not only traditional science fiction tropes but also a host of literary references and techniques (along with numerous cinematic allusions). Rather than imposing various literary allusions and styles onto an existing science fiction framework, however, and rather than simply writing literary fiction that just happens to include science fiction elements, Kessel is one of a handful of contemporary writers in the field who have achieved an effective synthesis of two disparate literary strands. As his work demonstrates, "science fiction" and "literature" are not mutually incompatible. Further, "literary science fiction" has two beneficial aspects beyond the pleasure readers derive from it. First, it shows that science fiction fans and writers need not resist the introduction of "literary" matters into the field, and second, it demonstrates that mainstream writers and critics who still are condescending toward science fiction are speaking from a position of increasingly inexcusable ignorance. One could even hope that science fiction writers such as Kessel might serve as a bridge between two literary worlds.

It is more or less a truism that writers are people who read a lot, or at least used to before they started writing themselves. Also, it has always been the case that science fiction writers tend to read not only frequently but also widely. Less common in the field, until recent decades, has been the science fiction writer who enters the profession not from a background in the sciences or from fandom (though both are still rather frequent) but from an academic background in literary studies and/or creative writing. Thus a quick glimpse at Kessel's curriculum vitae is relevant. After earning a bachelor's degree in English and physics and a master's and doctorate degree in English, he joined the faculty of North Carolina State University, where he teaches American literature and creative writing. To explore how Kessel unites a literary sensibility with science fiction, four examples will serve: his novel *Good News from Outer Space* (1989) and his stories "Invaders" (1990), "Buffalo" (1991), and "The Juniper Tree" (2000).

Both *Good News from Outer Space* and "Invaders" employ bizarrely behaving aliens as foils to highlight the foibles and darker sins of bizarrely behaving humans. In *Good News from Outer Space,* the setting is the premillennial United States, where a televangelist promises the appearance of Jesus in a spaceship and where tabloid journalists feed the public's hysterical fears. A setting, in other words, ripe for satire, one of Kessel's literary gifts. The satire is combined with a madcap plot of strange and funny incidents, such as the protagonist's wife joining a feminist terrorist group that plans to introduce a potion that will make men more like women, the detective hired to trail the protagonist believing instead her job is to assassinate him, or the aliens disguising themselves as the key human characters (again, as in Kessel's "Faustfeathers," the influence of the Marx Brothers is evident here). With its gonzo plotting and satirical bite, the novel is both hilarious and depressing, given how close to home much of Kessel's satire is.

Another of Kessel's gifts is his felicity with description, with both physical settings and characters. His depiction of the interior of a Baptist church in the American South, for instance, is superlative, as is his more imaginative description of what someone who has been revived from death might experience in the first moments after regaining consciousness. He also, for all of his comedic skills, ably portrays moments of great poignancy, as when an alien disguised as a human seduces a woman and literally brands her as a loser or when another alien seduces a minor-league baseball player and causes him to relive key moments from his past. In these richly realized characters, Kessel puts the lie to the idea that science fiction cannot deal with characters' internal conflicts and agonies as effectively as mainstream literary fiction can.

The aliens in Kessel's story "Invaders" also act in ways that are impossible for humans to fathom and that are not explained in the text. They land on Earth, and the first words spoken by the alien, dressed like the comic-book superhero the Flash, are "Cocaine. . . . We need cocaine."[16] The aliens then proceed to wreck the world economy, use artistic masterpieces as rugs, and coke themselves into oblivion, all for no apparent purpose. Kessel's satire of different human motivations, on the other hand, is sharp and clear, as in his depiction of a broker's dealings with the aliens, who wish to sell dollars (earned by selling their advanced scientific information on Earth) for francs—$50 billion worth of francs every week:

> Prescott thought about it. It would take every trick he knew —and he'd have to invent some new ones—to carry this off. The dollar was going to drop through the floor, while the franc would punch through the sell-stops of every trader on ten world markets. The exchanges would scream bloody murder. The repercussions would auger holes in every economy north of Antarctica. . . .
>
> Besides, it made no sense. Not only was it criminally irresponsible, it was stupid. The Krel would squander every dime they'd earned.
>
> Then he thought about the commission on $50 billion a week.
>
> Prescott looked across at the alien. From the right point of view, Flash resembled a barrel-chested undergraduate from Special Effects U. He felt an urge to giggle, a euphoric feeling of power. "When do we start?" (79)

In addition to such satirical passages, this excerpt also serves as an example of Kessel's attention to style. The writing is not pretentious or self-consciously literary, but it is obviously crafted, clearly the product of an author for whom style is part of the writing rather than something that, as in much earlier SF, should be invisible, merely a vehicle for the plot and the ideas.

Kessel's near-future story of inscrutable aliens mucking up human society is interleaved with another story, which draws on the materials of historical fiction rather than science fiction. It is the story of Pizarro's conquest of the Incas in the sixteenth century. Here it is the Europeans who are the invaders, the aliens who muck up another society, and thus Kessel implies that in a sense what the alien Krel do to Western culture parallels what Western culture did to non-Western cultures centuries earlier; in fact, it perhaps serves as payback for their actions.

The juxtaposition of historical fiction and science fiction in "Invaders" is enough to mark Kessel's story as postmodern, but in addition, the narrator intrudes into both narratives throughout the story to comment on his methods and to note parallels with his life. For instance, after the aliens request cocaine, the narrator writes, "I sit at my desk writing a science-fiction story. . . . In the morning I drink coffee to get me up for the day, and at night I have a gin and tonic to help me relax" (73). Later, after one of the sixteenth-century sections, he writes, "The part of this story about the Incas is as historically accurate as I could make it, but this Krel business is science fiction. I even stole the name 'Krel' from a 1950s SF flick. I've been addicted to SF for years" (81)—again making a connection between the various characters' addictions and his own, as does the note about how the Incas' descendants produce coca, which is converted to cocaine and sold to North Americans (and requested by alien invaders). The narrator's most telling connections between some of the story's major themes come in the last narrative intrusion. Noting that much science fiction has offered comforting escapes and power fantasies to readers who are often powerless, he says that SF could be considered "as much an evasion of reality as any mind-distorting drug." Alluding to the titles of some of SF's major magazines, he continues:

> The typical reader comes to SF at a time of suffering. He seizes on it as a way to deal with his pain. It's bigger than his life. It's astounding. Amazing. Fantastic. Some grow out of it; many don't. Anyone who's been around SF for a while can cite examples of longtime readers as hooked and deluded as crack addicts.
>
> Like any drug addict, the SF reader finds desperate justifications for his habit. SF teaches him science. SF helps him avoid "future shock." SF changes the world for the better. Right. So does cocaine. (92)

Yet despite these critiques of science fiction and of much of its faithful readership, the narrator allows that it does serve an important function:

> Having been an SF user myself, however, I have to say that, living in a world of cruelty, immersed in a culture that grinds people into fish meal like some brutal machine, with histories of destruction stretching behind us back to the Pleistocene, I find it hard to sneer at the desire to escape. Even if escape is delusion. (93)

In the story's striking conclusion, another figure of European descent appears among the sixteenth-century Incas, described as identical to the narrator's earlier description of himself: "The man spoke some foreign word. 'Goddamn,' he said in a language foreign to Timu, but which you or I would recognize as English. 'I made it'" (94). This time traveler, the narrator made flesh in his own story, then proceeds to prepare the Incas for the invaders who have not yet appeared, thus not only twisting the story further into postmodern territory but also driving it in the direction of alternate history: "When the first Spaniards landed on their shores a few years later, they were slaughtered to the last man, and everyone lived happily ever after" (94). Kessel's use of the clichéd concluding phrase is hardly a cliché here, however; rather, it is a final acknowledgment of fiction's artifice, the desire to rewrite the wrongs of the real world.

Alternate history also drives Kessel's 1991 story "Buffalo," which depicts a meeting in 1943 between the author's father, Jack Kessel, and H. G. Wells, a meeting that never took place. Otherwise, the story is almost entirely straight realism, alternating third-person limited omniscient points of view between the two "characters," with the climax coming with the working-class Jack Kessel awkwardly complimenting Wells on his work and Wells taking offense at being compared to Edgar Rice Burroughs, "the writer of pulp trash." The only deviation from realism, apart from the fact that this meeting never happened, comes with the author's occasional commentaries on the story and the two men, as well as his references to the fact that he is listening to the music of a third "character," Duke Ellington, who is performing with his band in the Washington, D.C., dance hall where Wells and Kessel's father meet.

It is Ellington's music, is fact, that allows Kessel to end the story on a positive note rather than with the despair both men in the story feel about their frustrated hopes and dreams. The music comforts both men and leads to an authorial comment about the nature of art. Earlier in the story Kessel had noted, perhaps unfairly, that for forty years Wells had "subordinated every scrap of his artistic ambition to promoting his vision" of revolutionary social and political change, and here at the end he writes:

> Through the music speaks a truth that Wells does not understand, but that I hope to: that art doesn't have to deliver a message in order to say something important. That art isn't always a means to an end but sometimes an end in itself. That art may not be able to change the world, but it can still change the moment.[17]

Thus Kessel echoes one of the themes of "Invaders," that art may be a form of escape but that it can serve an important function nonetheless.

More traditionally SF is Kessel's 2000 story "The Juniper Tree," the plot of which echoes the story of the same name told by the Brothers Grimm. The setting is a moon colony, where a man and his adolescent daughter relocate in order to start a new life. At first the man takes advantage of the colony's greater sexual license, but when his daughter does the same, the man has difficulty coming to terms with her blossoming sexuality. Thus the story, in addition to convincingly describing what life might be like on a moon colony and cleverly using a folktale as the basis for a science fiction story, is an effective portrayal of the father's selfishness and his feelings about his daughter's maturation.

Unfortunately, when people unfamiliar with written SF think of "science fiction," they are less likely to think of writers like Kessel and more likely to think about writers like Michael Crichton—smart, competent, and inventive but more concerned with writing fast-paced thrillers than with literary values. Crichton typically employs the materials of science fiction in popular novels that play upon contemporary concerns about various forms of scientific research and technology, often abused for corporate gain. Thus in *Jurassic Park* (1990), an effort to use genetic engineering to recreate dinosaurs on an island theme park runs amok in a morality tale about nature and human nature. Employing a multiple point-of-view technique that rushes readers through the plot while giving them little insight into the book's two-dimensional characters, *Jurassic Park* is science fiction in content but stands apart from the field in its sensibility. Rather than exploring the effects of change brought about by science and technology, as does most SF, Crichton's novel exploits fears about science and technology, which drive an exciting, action-packed story rather than being objects of serious consideration. As SF editor and publisher Charles N. Brown says,

> Thrillers, mysteries, commercial fantasy, and most other types of commercial fiction are consolatory by nature. They imply a wrongness in the world that has to be set right to return the world to the equilibrium point it started at before that wrongness. But SF says you can never put the genie back in the bottle. After the story, the world changes and changes and changes. This is also why SF won't usually sell in best-seller numbers: because it's not consolatory, and doesn't return the reader to a normal life.[18]

To be fair, though, the quality of Crichton's work is on a level with much of the work that has been produced by writers from within the genre, and he has a greater familiarity with and respect for SF than most other writers outside the field who wish to use the materials of SF for a metaphorical purpose. Yet one wishes that works that are less commercial, such as Frederik

Pohl's novel *The World at the End of Time,* published the same year as *Jurassic Park,* could find a larger readership, even if Crichton's best-seller status seems a distant dream for most SF writers.

Pohl's 1990 novel, like Spinrad's *Child of Fortune* or Simmons's *Hyperion Cantos* or his own "Day Million" (1966), could also be said to be a quintessential science fiction work, and not only because it includes many traditional SF motifs, such as aliens, space travel, colonization of other worlds, the effects of relativity, genetic engineering, and cryogenics. There are two main stories in *The World at the End of Time,* which converge at the novel's conclusion: the story of an effort to establish a colony on another world and the story of a powerful alien being that resides in stars. The book is very much in the tradition of hard SF, with explanatory discussions throughout about the composition of stars, the physics involved with interstellar travel, and how food could be produced on a starship, yet it is highly readable. In many ways, then, Pohl's novel is comparable to a type of eighteenth-century English literature known as Georgian or Georgic. As Donald M. Hassler has argued, science fiction is "a particularly modern Georgic form of writing" characterized by a "middle style" accessible to middle-class readers, "vivid imagery," and pedagogical content, especially regarding scientific concepts.[19] While Hassler's argument concerns Delany's *Dhalgren* (1975), the parallels he draws between the Georgic literature of the Augustan age and modern science fiction could apply to Pohl's novel as well.

The World at the End of Time is also very much an example of how science fiction can challenge conventional notions. For instance, on the new colony, having more people available sooner to help with the many tasks of building a new world is essential, so young people are encouraged to become parents soon after they are fertile, a throwback to earlier human patterns of reproduction but somewhat shocking for readers who live in a culture that encourages children to postpone having children until their late teens or later. Contrary to Kessel's claims about the arguments some SF readers produce to defend their addiction, readers of Pohl's *World at the End of Time* and comparable SF works can indeed learn something about science, be better prepared for radical change in the future, and simply expand their minds through encountering scientifically rigorous yet highly imaginative concepts.

Pohl's *World at the End of Time* is obviously a science fiction novel, from its content to its cover art. Less obviously SF on the surface, in both its content and cover art, Karen Joy Fowler's *Sarah Canary* (1991) is more subversive. The cover depicts a woman in nineteenth-century attire, and the novel is about a woman in the nineteenth-century United States, but the reading of *Sarah Canary* as science fiction depends entirely upon the question of who exactly this woman is.

The book is set in the late 1800s in the Pacific Northwest, where a woman who seems to be insane is found in a Chinese labor camp. A worker named Chin is assigned care of the woman, whose birdlike speech (if speech indeed it is) is incomprehensible, and he tries to help her reach an insane asylum. The woman is institutionalized and given the name Sarah Canary, but she manages to escape and takes up with Chin, along with a fellow inmate named B.J. and a progressive lecturer named Adelaide Dixon. The wanderers, after a series of picaresque adventures, eventually reach San Francisco, from where Chin returns to China and where Sarah disappears.

The novel thus reads like historical fiction, and indeed, one of the strengths of the book is Fowler's depiction of the setting in general and of her representatives of various disenfranchised groups in the late-nineteenth-century United States in particular. At the same time, there is the mystery of Sarah's identity, which is never clearly resolved. It is possible, certainly, to read *Sarah Canary* as realistic, yet more often readers and reviewers have picked up on the novel's suggestions that perhaps there is a fantastic explanation for Sarah's oddness and her abrupt appearance and disappearance. Some have suggested that *Sarah Canary* is a ghost story, or perhaps that Sarah is a vampire, but the more common fantastic reading of the novel identifies Sarah as an alien. If so, *Sarah Canary* is one of the most original first-contact stories in the history of science fiction, a story of alien contact in which it is not explicitly spelled out that the alien *is* an alien, and in which, echoing "The Women Men Don't See" by James Tiptree Jr. and *The Female Man* (1975) by Joanna Russ, the figure of the alien becomes a metaphor for the alienation of women in a patriarchal society.

Gender issues, in fact, have been important in Fowler's work from the beginning of her career. She broke into the field with "Recalling Cinderella" (1985), published by the Writers of the Future Contest, intended by its founder, science fiction writer L. Ron Hubbard, to promote new writers, and many of her early stories deal with gender. With Pat Murphy, she created the James Tiptree Jr. Award, which recognizes works of science fiction that deal significantly with gender issues. Yet it would be better to say that all of Fowler's fiction deals with a fundamental question: What does it mean to be human? For the most part she has dealt with this through works of fantasy and science fiction, but she has also achieved some success with mainstream fiction. While *Sarah Canary* sits on the border between realism and the fantastic, *The Jane Austen Book Club* (2004) is clearly realistic in intent. The book's positive reception—in contrast to the earlier struggles of some SF writers, most notably Philip K. Dick, to break into the mainstream—suggests that perhaps the boundaries dividing science fiction from literary fiction are no longer as difficult to cross as they once were.

A female protagonist is also at the center of Geoffrey A. Landis's Hugo-winning "A Walk in the Sun" (1991). She embarks upon a journey of her own, but this journey is one of survival, and "A Walk in the Sun" is a classic example of a science fiction problem story, a narrative in which the protagonist, typically using his or her scientific knowledge along with grace under pressure, must solve some significant problem. The problem for Landis's character is how to survive a crash landing on a lunar expedition before the life-support systems in her suit shut down. Employing the moon's lighter gravity and the suit's solar-powered abilities, she must in effect travel around the moon alone in a race against time. The story at once allows readers to observe how she thinks her way through the situation and what is going on in her head both intellectually and emotionally in the meantime. It is the type of story one can find only in science fiction.

Also more traditionally SF, displaying considerable imagination coupled with scientific rigor, is the work of Vernor Vinge, who like other writers of hard SF such as Gregory Benford, Joan Slonczewski, and Geoffrey A. Landis is a scientist as well as a science fiction writer. The central conceit of what has often been called Vinge's finest work, the 1992 novel *A Fire upon the Deep*, is that beyond the galaxy, once a species becomes intelligent enough to travel such great distances, it encounters a radically changed universe in which everything is faster: minds, bodies, vehicles, and the transmission of information. Vinge adroitly combines ambitious space opera with a host of conventional SF concepts, among them alien races, artificial intelligence, and advanced information technology, presented in unconventional ways. And again, as in much contemporary SF and contrary to the earlier ideas of SF's Golden Age, humanity is seen as of little importance in the larger scheme of things. Like many longer SF works of great complexity, such as Wolfe's *Book of the New Sun* and Simmons's Hyperion novels, it must be read to be fully experienced—as indeed is true of any literature worth reading.

Before launching into a series of books with a narrative line vaster in scale than even the great scope of *A Fire upon the Deep,* Neal Stephenson produced a number of well-crafted SF novels that stand alone, including the late cyberpunk novel *Snow Crash* (1992). Another "secret master" story, the plot involves a hacker who pays the bills by delivering pizzas but in the "metaverse" (Stephenson's version of cyberspace) uses his abilities to combat a dangerous computer virus. Like much cyberpunk fiction, it houses speculations about future interactions between humans and computers within the framework of the action-packed thriller. As in Kessel's work, there is also more than a touch of postmodernism here (for example, the main character's name is Hiro Protagonist).

Beyond the conventional cyberpunk concept, *Snow Crash* also offers an intriguing glimpse at the future direction of Stephenson's fiction, with conspiracies and its secret history of the world foreshadowing his later complex series that delves into the history of information in the modern world. Whether such novels are actually science fiction is a matter of debate, as are the boundaries of science fiction itself in the remainder of the 1990s and into the twenty-first century.

CHAPTER 5

Anything Goes,
1993–2000

In the early 1990s, Mars was in the air, so to speak. In 1990, Terry Bisson published a novel called *Voyage to the Red Planet,* in which a movie studio finances and films the first human voyage to Mars. The result is an interesting combination of hard SF and satire. Robert L. Forward's *Martian Rainbow* (1991) transposes tensions between the United States and Russia to Mars, while two 1992 novels, Jack Williamson's *Beachhead* and Ben Bova's *Mars,* also involve the first human exploration of the red planet and strive for scientific accuracy in imagining what might be involved in such a mission. Greg Bear's *Moving Mars* (1993), in contrast, concerns a twenty-second-century Martian colony that rebels against the government of Earth, and the colonization of Mars is also history in *Red Dust* (1993), a novel by British author Paul J. McAuley. And then there is Kim Stanley Robinson's Mars trilogy (1992–96), which encompasses a future history of the fourth planet from the sun ranging from colonization to political upheaval. Obviously, one can see something of the variety of American science fiction in the early 1990s, even within a few works with the same setting published within just years of one another.

Although the other novels have their merits (or, in some cases, serious problems with plot and character), it was Robinson's Mars books that were some of the most discussed and admired SF works of the early 1990s. His trilogy consists of *Red*

Mars (1992), *Green Mars* (1994), and *Blue Mars* (1996); additionally, related stories and documents are collected in *The Martians* (1999). According to Edward James, in the Mars books Robinson takes "the central tenet of science fiction—the extrapolation of current history—to greater lengths than any of his predecessors, and the Mars books are likely to be the touchstone of what is possible in the genre for a long time to come."[1]

Robinson accomplishes this task through his exploration, in meticulous, well-researched detail, of what a twenty-first-century manned voyage to Mars might entail and how the people on the mission might interact with one another under such conditions; of what they might encounter on the untamed surface of the planet once they land there; of how they might construct an underground base from which to begin their initial efforts to transform the planet through terraforming;[2] of the creation of the first colonies on the surface; and of the ensuing ethnic, social, political, religious, and economic conflicts as the Martian colonists strive to create a new world. Along the way, there is ample discussion of these issues, along with debates about the ecological and environmental impact of the human transformation of Mars. Thus Robinson's Mars trilogy is both an example of hard SF, with its rigorous and thorough depiction of the scientific and technological implications of trying to travel to and inhabit even the planet closest to Earth, and a text within the utopian tradition, with its lengthy discussions and debates about what kind of society the colonists should create. At the same time, Robinson's Mars novels are hardly the type of thing many outside the field fear when considering science fiction; though filled with considerable scientific detail and numerous discussions of social issues, the books also contain believable, interesting characters, and there is more to the plot than descriptions of scientific phenomena.

Thus one could consider Robinson's Mars books, like certain other texts discussed in chapter 4, a compendium of assorted science fiction trends and major motifs. Science is certainly central to the books, from the treatment of the difficulties of sending a manned mission to Mars to how they might survive once they get there to the even more daunting challenge of trying to remake a planet in Earth's image. Social concerns, often the material of science fiction, are also central to the expansive narrative. Additionally, Robinson deals with how the two interact, specifically, how politics affects the development and use of technology. What Russell Letson writes in his review of *Green Mars* could be applied to the trilogy as a whole: "The breadth of Robinson's interests makes for a dense and intellectually ambitious book: psychology, political-economic theory, history, the planetary sciences and ecology, and the interactions of all these."[3] Yet the "fiction" side of the sometimes uneasy equation of "science fiction" is not neglected, and unlike lesser works, which present two-dimensional characters and unrealistic plots, Robinson's Mars books develop their characters as real figures in realistic situations. As John Clute puts it in his review of *Red Mars,* "We believe in these people as deeply as it is possible to believe in marks on paper."[4]

Overall, Robinson's Mars trilogy could be taken as a mark of the maturity of American science fiction by the end of the twentieth century. It would be helpful, perhaps, to contrast his achievement with that of certain other examples of American SF that use Mars as a setting. In Edgar Rice Burroughs's novel *A Princess of Mars,*[5] for example, which began a lengthy series about the exploits of larger-than-life hero John Carter on the planet the Martian natives called Barsoom, the hero is whisked away to Mars from Earth as if by magic, and the story is essentially sword-and-sorcery fantasy with some scientific elements casually thrown in. "A Martian Odyssey" (1934) by Stanley G. Weinbaum, besides repudiating the cliché of monsters from Mars that started with H. G. Wells's *War of the Worlds,* also was an experiment in depicting truly alien aliens, whereas in Burroughs's Barsoom series the only things that distinguished Martians from humans were their red skin and the fact that the women were oviparous. In Weinbaum's story, however, next to nothing is said about how humans actually make it to Mars, and neither Burroughs nor Weinbaum was much of a stylist. Despite efforts such as Weinbaum's to provide a more scientifically plausible depiction of what life on Mars might be like (assuming that it existed at all, a suspension of disbelief necessary in reading much SF), romantic images of an alien yet anthropomorphic Mars persisted, as in Leigh Brackett's stories and novels featuring the red planet. Like Brackett, who depicted humans conquering an ancient Martian race, Ray Bradbury in the stories that comprise *The Martian Chronicles* (1950) shows readers a romantic vision of an alien world despoiled by human destructiveness. Bradbury's book is a linchpin in the history of American SF, praised for its lyricism by critics who normally abhorred the genre (unlike many previous SF writers, Bradbury *did* pay attention to style) but criticized by many in the field for favoring romanticism over scientific rigor. In contrast, Frederik Pohl's less lyrical but far more scientifically sound *Man Plus* (1976) shows a man becoming a cyborg to withstand the alien environment of Mars, just one of a number of novels and stories published since the 1950s that recognized that dealing with another planet would not be an easy task. And then there is Robinson's trilogy, which effectively merges scientific soundness with solid characterization and writing that is never jarring and has sometimes even been called beautiful. Such a work surely testifies to the fact that, among some writers at least, American science fiction has grown from its pulp-magazine origins to a maturity in which every aspect of the fiction is not only competent but also confident and assured.

Robinson's Mars books are also representative of the growing size of American SF books and series. Although not a new phenomenon, as was noted earlier, one sees in 1990s SF a growing number of trilogies and larger series, attributable in part to marketing demands and in part to the fact that writers such as Robinson were dealing with large, complex sets of ideas whose workings-out required hundreds if not thousands of pages. C. J. Cherryh's extensive Alliance-Union series, for example, contains shorter series, all of which are set in the same future history and are related to one another.[6] Another example is the fiction of Nancy Kress, who sometimes writes in trilogies, one of which, the Beggars trilogy, began with the thought-provoking *Beggars in Spain* (1993), itself a fix-up from a Hugo-winning story.[7]

Beggars in Spain begins with a simple premise that has far-reaching consequences: for a price, parents in the near future may have their unborn children genetically engineered so that they will be able to live without sleep, with no physical or psychological side effects. One of the first of these children is Leisha Camden, the daughter of a successful businessman who wants to give her every possible advantage. Indeed, as it turns out, Leisha and her fellow Sleepless, as they are soon called, not only use the additional one-third of their day to develop their intellects and abilities but also generally possess remarkable gifts and a no-nonsense focus on using them. Consequently, they soon outstrip the Sleepers, their term for the unaltered majority population, in almost every possible field. Kress's *Beggars in Spain,* then, combines extrapolation based on the relatively recent field of genetic engineering with a traditional type of science fiction motif, the superman story—a story about a person or group of persons possessing mental and/or physical abilities that transcend those of normal human beings. As in many such stories, *Beggars in Spain* grants considerable attention to how the ungifted majority sees the gifted minority as a threat, resulting in the persecution of the Sleepless. Matters only get worse when it is revealed that the Sleepless, due to their genetic alterations, age at a much slower rate than normal humans and are virtually free of illness and disease. As might be expected, in the face of widespread hatred the Sleepless band together, and a sizable number of them elect to live separately from the rest of humanity, first in New York state and then, following further harassment, in a space station orbiting Earth. In this station, a group of the Sleepless conducts some genetic experiments of their own on the next generation, not only making the children Sleepless but also accelerating their nervous systems so that they are even more mentally advanced than the first generations of Sleepless.

Yet Kress's is no simple superman story, but rather a sophisticated exploration of the possible consequences of the creation of a genetic elite and of the social and ethical implications of inequality. For starters, the novel implicitly asks whether it is right that those with economic advantages have access to medical technologies in a society in which many people lack even basic medical care, with the suggestion that the divide between haves and have-nots will only widen with advances in medicine. Related to this is the question of whether those who are blessed with superior gifts owe anything to those who are less fortunate. What obligation does one have, goes the argument that gives the novel its title, to the beggars in Spain? In Ayn Rand's *Atlas Shrugged* (1957), which shares its major themes with Kress's

Beggars trilogy, individualism is promoted as the highest virtue; superior individuals, Rand argued, should follow their own passions and as a result will do more for society as a whole than if they had used their talents directly to improve life for others. Similar sentiments are shared by many of the Sleepless, who are often cold and emotionless among one another and especially toward those some of them call the Beggars, the Sleepers whom many of them view with contempt.

Here, however, Kress provides a more sophisticated look at the ethical implications of superiority than that found in Rand's novel. It is obvious that Rand presents her superior main characters as heroic and admirable. (Whether readers find them so is another matter, depending upon how convinced they are by Rand's philosophy.) In contrast, Kress's Sleepless are more complex, both as characters—they are far more realistically depicted and developed than any of Rand's protagonists—and in the ways they are presented to readers. In addition to the limited empathy the Sleepless possess, they all have character flaws that make them quite human, and they often clash with one another as well as with the Sleepers. Further, while it is clear that Leisha is more admirable than the coldly calculating leader of the self-exiled Sleepless, she makes serious mistakes and the leader has her good points. This is a novel, in other words, in which certain people and the positions they take are obviously better or worse but in which ambiguity exists, in which ideas are presented through dialogue rather than monologue. Kress's superior humans, then, are not necessarily morally superior, a fact reinforced by the ways in which the mentally accelerated offspring of the exiled Sleepless challenge their elders, although they too are not presented as unambiguously superior, as is the case in Rand and in many superman SF stories.[8]

All of these factors, from the consideration of where genetically engineering may lead not just scientifically but also socially to the philosophical question of whether the haves owe anything to the have-nots, make Kress's *Beggars in Spain* a fine example of what many of SF's supporters talk about when they claim that science fiction is a literature of ideas. Yet the novel is neither didactic nor a philosophical dialogue dressed up as a novel, as the book also succeeds as a work of fiction, with believable characters who face situations that the future might present as well as the age-old problems and pleasures of living with other people. In this sense, *Beggars in Spain,* for all of its scientific content, also works on a literary level. Science fiction scholar Thomas D. Clareson once said that he believed science fiction in its own unique way dealt with two questions basic to all literature: "What does it mean to be human?" and "What does it mean to be humane?"[9] In its treatment of its characters and its central theme, *Beggars in Spain* deals admirably with both.

Similar themes are given a considerably different treatment in Harlan Ellison's novella *Mefisto in Onyx* (1993). Like Kress's Beggars trilogy, it provides an original treatment of a conventional SF motif, in this case the idea of paranormal talents. The narrator, a telepath, rarely uses his talents because he finds most people's minds unpleasant to explore. At the behest of a former girlfriend, who has fallen in love with a serial killer she helped to convict but who now believes he is innocent, he reluctantly agrees to investigate the matter, only to find that the killer is also a telepath who has used people for centuries by transferring his mind into others' bodies. Ellen Weil and Gary K. Wolfe have ably analyzed the novella's strengths and weaknesses in their book on Ellison, including its theme of making the most of the life that is given to you.[10] Like Leisha at the conclusion of *Beggars in Spain,* the narrator of *Mefisto in Onyx* at the conclusion of the story starts on a new path, one in which he will better use his gifts for the benefit of others.

In addition to his fiction, Ellison is also noteworthy in the history of contemporary American science fiction for his contributions as an editor, particularly of the taboo-breaking anthologies *Dangerous Visions* (1967) and *Again, Dangerous Visions* (1972), and for his criticism of the label "science fiction writer." Echoing the efforts of Kurt Vonnegut Jr. (discussed in chapter 4) not to be stuck within the SF ghetto, starting in the 1960s Ellison deliberately rejected the designation "science fiction writer" and strove to have the label removed from his books as well. A number of reasons led to these efforts. First, while much of Ellison's early work was indisputably science fiction and while he has continued to write science fiction in the later part of his career, as illustrated by *Mefisto in Onyx,* unlike many writers in the field he has not devoted himself exclusively to science fiction, and work in his prolific career has included fantasy, realistic fiction, and essays about a variety of subjects. Thus, he believes, to call him a science fiction writer is too limiting. But even if he wrote only science fiction, Ellison has argued that the label reinforces the marginalization of writers of science fiction and prevents them from finding a readership outside the field. To a certain extent Ellison has succeeded in his efforts to transcend the limitations of genre fiction, both in his work and in the way his work is published, although he has not received the same degree of attention in the literary world as has Vonnegut. Nor have, as he has pointed out, most other authors who write science fiction. For instance, while Ellison's story "The Man Who Rowed Christopher Columbus Ashore" (1992)—which contains fantasy elements Ellison would label "magic realism" (borrowing a term from Latin American literature)—was selected in 1993 by Louise Erdrich for inclusion in *The Best American Short Stories,* a series that had previously paid scant attention to science fiction, in his afterword to the story, Ellison lamented the fact that so many worthy SF writers had been ignored by the literary mainstream.

Despite a general disregard for science fiction by most writers of literary fiction, a small number of mainstream writers in North America and Great Britain have used science fiction in their work while avoiding being labeled science fiction writers. For instance, a British writer such as H. G. Wells could have a successful career as a realistic novelist despite the fact that his best-known works were what were called at the time "scientific romances." Similarly, the literary reputations of later British authors such as Aldous Huxley, George Orwell, C. S. Lewis, Anthony Burgess, William Golding, Doris Lessing, Kingsley Amis, and Iain Banks were not appreciably harmed by the fact that they occasionally (and sometimes famously) wrote what is indisputably science fiction.[11] In contrast, Canadian writer Margaret Atwood has assiduously avoided having novels that are clearly science fiction, such as *The Handmaid's Tale* (1985) and *Oryx and Crake* (2003), labeled as science fiction, precisely because, like Vonnegut and Ellison, she is aware of the negative consequences of such labeling. Philip K. Dick, one of the greatest talents American SF has ever produced, knew this all too well, as he found his mainstream efforts hampered by his label as a science fiction writer. It is little wonder, then, that when mainstream American writers venture into science fiction they often consciously distance themselves from the genre, as do their publishers. Often, in the opinion of many in the SF field, this is

just as well, as SF written by outsiders frequently shows an ignorance of what has already been done within the field and an
inability to deal with SF materials effectively. Yet occasionally,
mainstream American writers have written successful science
fiction. Three examples from the end of the twentieth century
are Richard Powers's *Galatea 2.2* (1995), *The Sparrow* (1996)
by Mary Doria Russell, and *Lives of the Monster Dogs* (1997)
by Kirsten Bakis.

The title of Powers's *Galatea 2.2* fuses classical mythology
—Galatea is the name given to the ideal woman, first created by
the sculptor Pygmalion and then brought to life by the goddess
Venus—with information technology, in which successive ver-
sions of software are numbered. Powers also combines a postmodern take on contemporary realism—although the novel is
set in the here and now, the protagonist is also named Richard
Powers and shares many biographical details with the author
—with a common science fiction theme, artificial intelligence.
Powers the character is invited to serve as resident humanist at
his former university and becomes involved with a scientist
named Lentz, who is attempting to program a computer so that
it could pass for human in a blind test—specifically, by being
able to pass a literature exam. However, as the computer gains
in intelligence, it also achieves awareness. As is usual in such SF
stories, Powers the author presents readers with an intriguing
idea—can machines think?—and a set of corresponding questions: If machines think, are they alive? Do they, like their sentient human creators, have rights? And are we humans also
merely carbon-based machines with brains that differ from
computers only in chemical structure? In addition, *Galatea 2.2*
expands these themes into other parts of the story, such as par-
alleling the protagonist's frustrating efforts to learn Dutch while

living in the Netherlands and connecting Lentz's obsession to his wife's dementia.

Powers's *Galatea 2.2* thus offers an unusual sort of SF reading experience. Some American SF novels are as deliberately "literary," but the focus of *Galatea 2.2* is distinctly different. While the accomplishment of artificial intelligence is a key part of the novel, it is not as central to the narrative as it would be in a traditional work of science fiction; and while many SF novels develop characters as fully as is typical in literary fiction, Powers, like most writers of literary fiction, makes the exploration of character the true center of the book. The scientific component is not neglected, and it is obvious that both Powers the author and Powers the character are fascinated by the possibilities of artificial intelligence and that he (they?) has done his homework, but characterization simply counts for more—more than idea or plot, two of the most important aspects of most science fiction.

If Powers approaches the materials of science fiction in *Galatea 2.2* from the perspective of a self-professed humanist and former computer programmer, Mary Doria Russell entered the field by means of anthropology, in which she holds a doctoral degree, and religion, which is the central theme of her first two novels, *The Sparrow* and its sequel, *Children of God* (1998). A professed SF reader, Russell draws upon certain influences in *The Sparrow,* particularly the anthropological SF of Ursula K. Le Guin; and the structure of the novel, with chapters alternating between present and past, parallels that of Le Guin's *Dispossessed.* However, Russell comes to the field as an outsider. She chose science fiction, as she has said in interviews, only because she wanted to write a story in which people are confronted with a radically different culture for the first time. As this can no longer happen on Earth, she took the story into space.

The chapters of *The Sparrow* set in the story's "present," well into the twenty-first century, concern Emilio Sandoz, a Jesuit priest who has been traumatized by his experiences as part of an expedition to a relatively nearby planet from which signs of intelligent life were detected over four decades earlier. (Due to the effects of relativity, only a few years have passed for Emilio, while over forty years have elapsed on Earth.) As his friends and superiors try to help him recover from his physical and psychological wounds and to learn what happened to the expedition, the alternating chapters set in the story's "past" (which begins in the early twenty-first century) reveal how Emilio came to know the people who would compose the expedition: the radio astronomer who detected an alien song on a satellite dish in Emilio's native Puerto Rico; the couple who introduced them, a physician and her retired engineer husband, whom Emilio first met in Cleveland while teaching at a university there; the Jesuit priest who turned Emilio's life around, along with two Jesuit scientists; and a highly intelligent young woman who learns others' jobs so that the knowledge can be computerized. This unlikely crew, with funding from the Roman Catholic Church, transforms a mining asteroid into a spacecraft and heads for the Alpha Centauri system, following the Jesuit ideal of attaining knowledge.

Once they locate the planet from which the transmissions came, they encounter not one but two intelligent alien species, each with its own language and culture. Although Emilio is a proficient linguist and enables the expedition to communicate with the aliens, and although they learn certain aspects of the aliens' cultures, the story hinges on the fact that their understanding is simply too limited to cope with societies that are almost entirely foreign to them, with tragic results. Yet for all its dark and disturbing material, *The Sparrow* is a hopeful and even humorous novel. The humor derives from Russell's characters, very different individuals who nonetheless are smart, decent, and often very funny. The hopeful mood is a more complicated matter, intertwined as it is with the terrible events that lead to Emilio's religious crisis. The religious issues raised by *The Sparrow* are not entirely resolved by the novel's conclusion and are explored further in *Children of God,* but the novel's serious (yet not solemn) treatment of religious faith is subtle and sophisticated. Along with its characterization and its use of the common SF theme of first contact and the attendant difficulties of understanding an alien culture, the treatment of religious faith is one of the qualities that contributes to the effectiveness of *The Sparrow.* It is also interesting for its treatment of gender, which earned it the SF field's Tiptree Award.

Russell's relationship to the SF field, in fact, is another thing that makes *The Sparrow* an interesting example of American SF in the 1990s. While readily confessing that she admires a great deal of science fiction, she has been reluctant to identify herself as a science fiction writer, perhaps for reasons similar to those motivating authors such as Vonnegut and Ellison, and in fact her third novel is a work of historical fiction. Additionally, her initial efforts to publish *The Sparrow,* her first novel, were frustrated by agents and publishers who were hesitant about either the SF qualities of the book or its premise. After multiple rejections, the novel was picked up by a mainstream publisher and promoted simply as fiction, not science fiction. Neither the title, which alludes to Matthew 10:29–31 and its parallel passage in Luke, nor the cover art nor the genre indications on the book's spine and back cover gave any indication that this was a work of science fiction, and unlike many SF books of comparable quality, *The Sparrow* was a selection of the Book-of-the-Month

Club and became a frequent selection of the book-discussion groups that began to emerge at the end of the twentieth century.

While the response to Russell's novel was generally positive outside the SF field, within it reactions were mixed. Some faulted the novel for the ease with which Emilio and the rest of the expedition detect an alien culture, which just happens to be in a galaxy relatively close to ours, and travel there, in contrast with the painstakingly realistic depictions of just how hard it would be to get to Mars in the fiction of writers such as Ben Bova and Kim Stanley Robinson. Others within the field found in Russell yet another outsider who wanted to write science fiction but did not want to be called a science fiction writer. Yet many SF readers and critics admired *The Sparrow,* and some even proclaimed it one of the best works of American SF in the 1990s. The granting of the Tiptree Award was only one mark of its acceptance by many in the SF community.

Less successful in this regard was Kirsten Bakis's *Lives of the Monster Dogs,* which also appeared from a mainstream publisher and was not labeled as science fiction. In this case, though, the cover art clearly revealed its fantastic content, with its depiction of a well-dressed canine standing upright. What makes this science fiction rather than fantasy is the novel's description of how the intelligent dogs are the product of science, echoing H. G. Wells's *Island of Doctor Moreau* (1896), rather than of magic, as in animal fantasy. The premise is that surgically altered dogs, who are aided as well with mechanical voices and hands, arrive in New York in the early twenty-first century and take Manhattan by storm with their artistic and intellectual accomplishments. Yet as in Wells and Mary Wollstonecraft Shelley's *Frankenstein* (another obvious influence), the creatures' ideas about what they want differ from those of the men who would control them. Despite the novel's title, however, this is not a story about monsters but rather, as in Powers's *Galatea 2.2* and Russell's *Sparrow,* about the desire for love and meaning. *Lives of the Monster Dogs* is a poignant tale of yearning and loss.

Emotional depth, however, is not the sole province of mainstream literary fiction; for all its focus upon matters of plot and concept, science fiction is often capable of presenting readers with well-developed, credible characters whose conflicts are both convincing and moving, especially in the age of maturity represented by the last three decades of the twentieth century. As representative figures, consider two authors working within the genre, the veteran Joe Haldeman (born 1943) and the newer writer Ted Chiang (born 1967).

Haldeman's early masterpiece, *The Forever War* (discussed in chapter 2), has often been praised as one of the most effective works of military SF ever written, both for its convincing presentation of how warfare might be conducted in the future and for its depiction of the effects of warfare, future or present, upon those who experience it firsthand. In the 1990s, Haldeman returned to military SF, albeit with a sophistication often lacking in popular examples of the form, with *Forever Peace* (1997). Although thematically similar to *The Forever War,* it is not a sequel to that book, unlike his next novel, *Forever Free* (1999). In *Forever Peace,* the setting is the mid-twenty-first century, and the conflict is on Earth rather than in outer space, between humans of the industrialized Alliance and humans of the Third World. Yet the people who fight for the Alliance do so from a distance, using robot warriors controlled remotely by humans beings jacked in (the influence of cyberpunk is evident here)[12] who share in a group mind during the experience. The protagonist, a physicist named Julian Class, is one such "soldier," and like Mandella from *The Forever War,* his experiences lead him to pursue his own agenda. Haldeman develops his depiction of a near-future United States well, and his implicit critique of the abuses of military power is as effective as anything by Frederik Pohl—as is Haldeman's portrayal of a fundamentalist Christian group called the Hammer of God, also known as the Enders for their desire for the end of the world. The end indeed may come, though not from a religious cause but a scientific one, as Class's lover has learned that Jupiter, due to a scientific project gone awry, may be on the verge of reenacting the Big Bang. Another strength of the novel is its employment of the devices of hard SF, from astrophysics to nanotechnology, all without impinging upon the story or its characters. And it is Haldeman's presentation of Class's personal struggles that in the end makes the novel worth reading, as does his technique of alternating between first-person and third-person points of view.

Also sophisticated in terms of technique and in its emotional depth is Ted Chiang's "Story of Your Life" (1998). As in Russell's *Sparrow,* a linguist is called upon to facilitate communication with aliens, only here the aliens have come to Earth. Remaining in orbit, the aliens establish a network of visual and audio connections, and an anxious military has reluctantly called in scholars and scientists like the protagonist to try to learn more about their unexpected visitors. As the linguist, after far more difficulty than experienced by Emilio in *The Sparrow,* slowly comes to grasp aspects of the aliens' language, she learns that they experience time simultaneously rather than sequentially, as humans do. Following the idea that language shapes the way we think, the linguist, immersed in this alien form of communication, also begins to experience past, present, and future as one.[13] This then relates to the technical accomplishment of the story, in which the protagonist addresses her unborn daughter, relating both the story of her experiences with the aliens and events that will occur in her child's life and in her own future. The result, besides being a thought-provoking SF story, is both structurally appealing and emotionally affecting. In the parts of the story dealing with the protagonist's relationships with friends and family and especially her yet-to-be-born daughter, Chiang succeeds in writing a story as richly developed in characterization as any mainstream story published in a literary magazine.

One would think, given writers such as Chiang and given the increasing maturity of the better examples of American science fiction as a whole, that the boundaries between science fiction and the mainstream would show increasing signs of blurring, but this has hardly been the case, as SF continues to be marginalized in various ways. Yet some signs of blurring are evident, not only with mainstream writers such as Powers, Russell, and Bakis drawing upon the materials of science fiction in their work but also with the work of certain SF writers blending more and more into the realm of the mainstream. Notable examples of this development are the novels of the late 1990s and early 2000s written by Neal Stephenson, who began his career with ecological SF works, then shifted into cyberpunk, and then started writing novels that are much more difficult to categorize.

The starting point of the latter phase of Stephenson's career is *Cryptonomicon* (1999), although hints of the direction the novel takes may be seen in *The Diamond Age* (1995), with its conflation of history and science. But unlike this earlier novel, *Cryptonomicon* is set not in the future but in the past and the present, and not in a different past and present as in alternate history, but in a meticulously researched, realistically depicted past and present. Nevertheless, some have argued, most notably

John Clute, that with its focus on the implications of information technology, which is central to the novel, *Cryptonomicon* is as much a work of science fiction as historical fiction:

> *Cryptonomicon* is a novel about the world, a radical recasting of history since the Second World War as a conspiracy of data; and it could be argued that any novel which is about the world shares a structural identity with the most overt tale of sf. Sf is that set of stories, more precisely, which *argues* the world; which argues the *case* of the world. It is important and likely, but not necessary, that that argument promulgates outcomes that have not yet become the case in reality. That *Cryptonomicon* is set in the past of the world is inessential in any argument that understands it, correctly, as an sf text about understanding the world as a set of instructions the world must adhere to.[14]

Thus, while the related narratives of the novel focus on a code breaker during World War II and his grandson, a contemporary computer programmer working in Asia, in many respects *Cryptonomicon* is a secret history of the impact of information on the modern world. It is also, given its nature, a book that blurs the boundaries between mainstream fiction and science fiction, and it was received as such, reviewed in the standard SF venues as well as in publications such as the *New York Times Book Review.*

Gary K. Wolfe presents a similar argument to Clute's, linking Stephenson's *Cryptonomicon* with Bruce Sterling's *Zeitgeist* (2000) and saying that both novels "bear all the hallmarks of good near-future science fiction—the world slightly estranged from our own by new developments in technology and exaggerated social trends, the elements of absurdist social satire, the sense of history as malleable—but in fact," he continues, "neither novel is even set in the future nor makes much use of the surface machinery of science fiction."[15] Wolfe adds, "Both novels, however, are rife with the science fictional habits of treating speculative thought as though it were heroic action, and of manipulating ideas as though they were characters."[16] Here Wolfe supports an idea that has long been held by many critics about science fiction, that it is not so much a genre with established story formulas, as in mystery fiction and romance novels, or with certain expected elements, as in the western, but rather a mode, a way of thinking about ideas within a fictional context.

Stephenson's ambitious novel, which unites science and fiction in a way that does not exactly conform to conventional notions of what science fiction is yet to many readers *feels* like science fiction, offers a good example of what some critics, most notably Wolfe, have said when discussing the increasingly blurry line between science fiction and both contemporary mimetic fiction and the other fantastic genres, fantasy and horror. For instance, to draw upon examples cited by Wolfe, the contemporary novels of Jonathan Carroll freely combine horror, fantasy, and science fiction elements, while Jonathan Lethem's *Gun, with Occasional Music* (1994) is a detective story set in the early twenty-first century that includes cartoonish talking animals.[17] The result, Wolfe notes elsewhere, is that science fiction has influenced other genres and in turn been influenced by them, leading to what he calls an "evaporation" of science fiction (along with fantasy) into the literary and cultural landscape, by which he means not that it is vanishing but that it is infiltrating literary and cultural expressions outside the genre.[18]

Yet Wolfe does not suggest that such a "destabilization" of science fiction and other fantastic genres is universal:

> While on one end of the spectrum are writers who strive to liberate genre materials from genre constraints, and in the vast center are authors who work with varying degrees of contentment within a genre, testing its possibilities without contesting its terms, there are at the other end writers for whom genre seems to be its own reference point, if not very nearly the whole of the literary universe. . . . Science fiction writers who periodically proclaim the impending death of that genre cite as major culprits the flood of novelizations and franchises based on properties such as *Star Trek, Star Wars,* or *The X-Files,* which, it is claimed, divert the skills of talented novelists from their own work and crowd more imaginatively challenging science fiction off the bookstore shelves.[19]

Some in the field would second these views. Regarding the dominance of fantasy over science fiction and of the increased number of tie-ins, for instance, British SF writer and historian Brian Stableford writes, "The summation of all these trends implies that the more earnest and thoughtful kinds of science fiction are in danger of being removed altogether from the commercial arena."[20] However, says Wolfe, commercialism has not seemed to hurt SF to any great extent and may have even helped it, although certain types of less commercial publications, such as experimental work and collections of short stories, have been relegated to smaller independent publishing companies. "Of greater concern than simple commercialism," he says, "is the increasing self-referentiality of many genre texts, a narrowing of horizons that eventually leads to an accelerating inward spiral, resulting in a kind of genre implosion or collapse—virtually the opposite of the volatility represented by the more innovative or adventurous writers."[21] Such an implosion, Wolfe says, would not necessarily mean a genre such as SF would disappear or cease to be profitable, but that it would lead to a lessening of creativity and a decrease in readership. Whether this will happen to science fiction remains to be seen.

Wolfe's statements about the diversity of science fiction at the end of the twentieth century are echoed by SF writer and editor Gardner Dozois, who in his summations of developments within SF in his annual *Year's Best Science Fiction* anthologies for the closing years of the 1990s and the beginning of the 2000s repeatedly commented upon how, despite some claims to the contrary, not only was science fiction not dead or dying, but that there was more science fiction being published than ever before, much of it excellent. For example, in his essay about the state of SF in 2000, he writes that the field is doing well commercially and that "artistically, even taking into account all of the tie-ins and media and gaming-associated books that crowd the shelves, there are still considerably *more* science fiction novels of quality being published now than were being published in, say, 1975 (including a few that would probably not have been *allowed* to be published at all back then), in a very wide range of styles and moods, by a spectrum of writers ranging from Golden Age giants to Young Turks with one book under their belts—quite probably more quality material (including a wide range of short work) than any one reader is going to be able to *read* in the course of one year."[22]

Dozois's summation stands as an excellent overview of the state of American SF at the end of the twentieth century, but implicit in his summation and explicit in Wolfe's argument is a view that may seem entirely obvious but often is not seen as such by critics outside the field: the idea that science fiction possesses a great deal of variety not only in content and in style but also in quality, that "science fiction" is merely a description of what readers can expect to find in any given story and not a marker of quality that adequately tells readers whether the story is poor, excellent, or somewhere in between.

CHAPTER 6

Conclusion

The Age of Maturity

One of the many definitions of science fiction that has been offered by critics and historians of the form is that, with the exception of such subtypes as prehistoric fiction and alternate histories, it is fiction that is concerned with the future. It seems entirely appropriate, then, that those within the field of science fiction are concerned about its own future. In an age in which much of what was written about in older science fiction is now reality—more than one commentator has remarked that we live in a science fiction world—and in which science fiction appears regularly on television (both programs and commercials), in movie theaters, and in other media (most particularly the Internet, that most science fictional entity of contemporary life), does science fiction literature have a future? In a time in which publishing has become increasingly commercial, in which best sellers dominate the shelves of mammoth chain bookstores, and in which readers are declining in numbers and forecasters predict the emergence of a "postliterary" visual culture, what kind of future is there for science fiction literature?

Of course, most science fiction writers and readers have tended to downplay the ability of science fiction to predict the future accurately; at best, they say, science fiction offers possible future scenarios. Consequently, their comments on current directions in the field and the future viability of the form are little more than informed speculation. It is interesting to note, though, that by and large writers are sounding more and more pessimistic, for reasons addressed at the end of chapter 5. Less frequently given as a reason for that sense of pessimism but arguably just as important is the continued lack of respect for science fiction, despite the high quality of many of its works and decades of academic attention.

Octavia E. Butler, John Crowley, Karen Joy Fowler, Joe Haldeman, John Kessel, Kim Stanley Robinson, Connie Willis, and Gene Wolfe, to name but a few, are some of the best writers working in the United States today. Yet their work is largely unknown, not only by most Americans but also by most critics and professors of literature. The reason for their relative anonymity is simply that these writers work primarily or entirely in science fiction. In the thirty years between 1970 and 2000, when literary canons expanded tremendously to include previously marginalized female and minority writers as well as texts other than fiction, poetry, or drama, science fiction has remained either unnoticed or considered en masse as sub-literary by the majority of critics and professors.

This relative neglect is baffling, given that many American science fiction writers are as capable of producing works of high literary quality as authors of literary fiction. Not all SF is of high quality, of course. To return to Sturgeon's Law, a substantial amount of work in the genre is poor or mediocre—like most things. Yet most critics do not look at, say, television comedy as a set of shows all of equal value, but rather as a spectrum ranging from the most formulaic and unfunny show that is justifiably canceled after three episodes to the sublime satire of *The Simpsons*. Similarly, science fiction is not a homogeneous body of writing but a spectrum ranging from works written by tin-eared authors with unoriginal ideas, unbelievable plots, and two-dimensional characters to the work of the authors listed above and those of comparable quality. Yet as Theodore Sturgeon said, science fiction tends to be judged by its worst examples.[1]

To be fair, the field shares part of the blame for this problem, as there is a strong antiliterary attitude within American science fiction. One of the better known graffiti in the history of science fiction is the following, reputedly scrawled on a chalkboard at a Worldcon during the 1970s: "Let's take science fiction out of the classroom and put it back in the ghetto where it belongs!" This is but one example of the attitude, common among fans and writers alike, that science fiction is different from other types of fiction, especially that found in the "mainstream," that science fiction should not be judged by the same standards as other types of fiction, and that the values of science fiction are, in fact, completely different from so-called literary values—and not only different, many have claimed, but better. As SF critic Gary K. Wolfe has written, SF has often seemed to be

a kind of literature that insisted on repeatedly shooting itself in the foot. It was a field that chronically complained that no one took it seriously, yet it seemed to make precious few efforts to take *itself* seriously. . . . It muttered about itself ceaselessly in letter columns and fanzines, but made few efforts to engage the larger world, and when it did it was often in the form of idealistically naïve manifestoes making the fatal claim that SF was not only worth reading, but that it was the *only* thing worth reading.[2]

As noted earlier, the history of this attitude is lengthy, going back at least to the split between romanticism and realism in the nineteenth century, the association of science fiction with an emergent popular culture in the early twentieth century, and the associated disdain of the dominant modernist aesthetic for the artifacts of popular culture. As Wolfe has said, "The act of reading fantastic literature became marginalized not only ideologically, by virtue of its content, but commercially, by virtue of its venues of publication," specifically, the pulp magazines and paperback books in which so much of American science fiction was first published.[3] Other contributing factors, as discussed in chapter 4, include internal divisions in SF caused by its use in the classroom and the controversy over the literary aspirations of the New Wave.

Despite the emergence of some successes in American SF outside the field by the mid-twentieth century—such as Walter M. Miller Jr.'s *Canticle for Leibowitz,* Robert A. Heinlein's *Stranger in a Strange Land,* or the work of the popular Ray Bradbury—the general reputation of American science fiction remained poor into the 1970s, regardless of the efforts of the New Wave writers, who chafed at the critical and commercial limitations of the genre and challenged many of its longstanding conventions.

Since these writers desired to escape the science fiction ghetto, and since they employed more literary techniques than many American science fiction writers before them, why did they fail? Why did science fiction fail to break through to a larger audience? Why did the stigma of the science fiction label, though weaker than in earlier decades, remain?

In part, the New Wave failed because it was short lived and most of the writers associated with the movement turned their attention to other matters. In addition, many of the concerns and approaches of the New Wave were appropriated by writers not affiliated with it, from older writers such as Frederik Pohl to younger writers who were more traditional, such as Larry Niven. Also, other new things came along to occupy the attention of the American science fiction community, such as the influx of female writers; the emergence of hard science fiction, firmly rooted in the physical sciences; and trends such as cyberpunk in the 1980s and alternate history in the 1990s. Sales were generally good and there was a lot of interesting work in the field, so fewer and fewer continued to worry about science fiction's literary reception. Still, there are many who feel that science fiction continues to be attacked or dismissed unfairly as subliterary, especially among those who practice a decidedly literary type of science fiction, which draws more or less equally from both science fiction traditions and the mainstream heritage.

All of this begs the question, what is literature? Answers to this question range from the inclusive to the limited, from the notion that all texts, written or oral, are literature to a more restricted view, that literature consists solely of the very best writing. Consider, for instance, the recent debate over Tom Wolfe's novel *A Man in Full* (1998). The book was attacked by both Norman Mailer and, more pointedly, John Updike, who in his *New Yorker* review claimed that Wolfe's novel, despite its ambition, "still amounts to entertainment, not literature, even literature in a modest aspirant form."[4]

Such a dismissal has consistently been made of science fiction throughout its history. It may be entertaining, its detractors say, and it may aspire to literary status, but it is still not literature. This attitude is puzzling, given that writers such as those listed at the beginning of the chapter demonstrate as much mastery over language, plot, characterization, setting, structure, style, and theme as their mainstream peers. Nor are these writers the exceptions that prove the rule. Instead, they are among the many writers currently working in American science fiction whose work exhibits all the hallmarks of what most would concur constitutes literature if these hallmarks were found outside of genre fiction.

Yet SF continues for the most part to be excluded from books and other resources dealing with contemporary American fiction. Consider, for instance, the histories of American literature published by the Columbia University Press. The comprehensive volume in the series, *Columbia Literary History of the United States* (1988), edited by Emory Elliott, understandably devotes little attention to science fiction since even a history of twelve hundred pages that attempts to cover the entire literary history of the country can say little about any given subject. A few pages are also devoted to science fiction in *The Columbia History of the American Novel* (1991), also edited by Elliott, although fewer than one might expect in such a lengthy and more focused work. Even more surprising is the omission of any chapters on genre fiction, including science fiction, in *The Columbia Companion to the Twentieth-Century American Short Story* (2000), edited by Blanche H. Gelfant, although there are chapters as specific as "The Ecological Short Story" and "The American Working-Class Short Story." And while Gelfant's volume does include author entries for SF writers Ray Bradbury and Ursula K. Le Guin, the omission of other notable authors of SF short stories, such as those by Theodore Sturgeon and Harlan Ellison, is glaring, nor is there an entry on John Crowley, one of the handful of contemporary American SF writers listed in the appendices to Harold Bloom's *The Western Canon* (1994).[5] (On the other hand, Bloom has edited several volumes concerning American SF writers in his numerous collections of criticism published by Chelsea House.)[6] Novels by Le Guin and Joanna Russ are briefly mentioned in Malcolm Bradbury's revised edition of *The Modern American Novel* (1992), but as examples respectively of feminist fiction and lesbian fiction, not as science fiction. In contrast, *The Salon.com Reader's Guide to Contemporary Authors* (2000), edited by Laura Miller with Adam Begley, includes an essay by SF critic John Clute called "Of This World: Why Science Fiction Can't Be Dismissed," and the May 2004 issue of *PMLA* was devoted to science fiction and literary studies. Also, Oxford University Press's *Good Fiction Guide* (2001), edited by Jane Rogers, includes a chapter on SF by British novelist Livi Michael and several entries on SF writers, as do *The Oxford Companion to Women's Writing in the United States* (1995), edited by Cathy N. Davidson and Linda Wagner-Martin, and *The Oxford Companion to African American Literature* (1997), edited by William L. Andrews, Frances Smith Foster, and Trudier Harris.

Even if Sturgeon's Law is correct and 90 percent of science fiction is crap, the talented tenth at the top would still offer an abundance of quality SF, to a degree unacknowledged by many literary critics and historians. Thus one must turn to cultural factors to explain the continued exclusion of science fiction from the highest ranks of American letters. One place to begin would be literature anthologies designed for use in college classrooms.

In July 1999, Elaine Showalter, whose well-known study *A Literature of Their Own: British Women Novelists from Brontë to Lessing* (1977) contributed to feminist efforts to promote the inclusion of lesser-known women writers in the literary canon, published an essay in the *Chronicle of Higher Education* describing her recent efforts to teach graduate assistants at

Princeton University how to teach. Among the most interesting parts of the essay are those that briefly describe her students' first classroom experiences with undergraduates. One, for instance, "was startled when her students declared that Margaret Atwood's *The Handmaid's Tale* was full of 'corny images we've all encountered in a million novels.'"[7] Apparently, though, the graduate student had not encountered such images before, or she would not have been so startled by her students' reactions. The likely reason is that she came to Atwood's dystopian novel after reading other works by the Canadian author, no doubt learning of her through college courses, while her first-year students likely read the novel in the context of a familiarity with SF, a type of writing the graduate student easily could have avoided throughout years of undergraduate and graduate study. Showalter's student at Princeton was probably startled because she doubtless thought *The Handmaid's Tale* was strikingly original, while anyone with any familiarity with science fiction would recognize that in many respects, as mainstream authors so often do when venturing into science fiction territory, Atwood was reinventing the wheel.

While many students from a variety of majors enter a science fiction class with considerable interest in the subject, having read extensively if not always widely in the field, a substantial minority are English majors taking the class either as an elective or out of a genuine curiosity (or perhaps both). Casey, one student from a winter 1999 science fiction course at Shawnee State University, was an example of the latter type of student. She was a senior middle-school education major with a concentration in English. Under her program requirements at the time, this meant that she had taken many English classes, as opposed to classes for a predominantly education curriculum.

She was bright, articulate, and reasonably well read. However, in this, her senior year at college, she had never before been exposed to science fiction. As it turned out, she actually had read some of the assignments in other English classes, in particular Daniel Keyes's "Flowers for Algernon" (1959) and Kurt Vonnegut Jr.'s "Harrison Bergeron" (1961). But these had not been presented to her as science fiction. In fact, Casey, like Showalter's student at Princeton, had managed to go through four years as an English major without ever being exposed to science fiction as a specific type of writing. Once one examines some of the popular anthologies used in English classes across the country, it is easy to understand why.

There is only so much any editor can cram into such anthologies, especially considering their extensive scopes; even given tissue-thin pages, small type, and lengths of over two thousand pages, some selections must be made. One cannot expect to find the entire Library of Congress in just one book. Moreover, while theoretical and social approaches to the study of literature and culture are valuable, most professors of literature (whether they would admit it or not) tend to believe that part of the selection principle for anthologies should be based on aesthetic considerations and that some writers are simply better than others. Thus most scholars take it as a matter of course that even the mega-anthologies omit some authors for both practical and evaluative reasons. What is problematic is the tacit assumption that such anthologies contain little to no modern science fiction simply because science fiction is not good enough to include. This returns to the question of how "literature" is defined, and it is instructive to consider briefly what John Updike, that most-canonical and most-anthologized author, has said on the subject in two book reviews.

First, Updike clearly has views on what is literature and what is not that transcend simple matters of genre, as is evident in his review of Wolfe's *Man in Full*. Though he praises certain aspects of the novel and terms it "high-minded," certain other aspects, along with Updike's claim that "the novel tries too hard to please us," lead him to the assertion that "*A Man in Full* still amounts to entertainment, not literature, even literature in a modest aspirant form."[8]

A clearer idea of what for Updike constitutes literature and what distinguishes it from other types of fiction, poetry, drama, and nonfiction can be gleaned from his review of *The World Treasury of Science Fiction,* a 1989 anthology edited by David G. Hartwell. Updike notes early in the essay that "science fiction has been around long enough, abundantly and variously enough, to keep even a mega-anthology like this one from offering a launching platform broad enough for generalizations that will go into lasting orbit." He even concedes that Hartwell "has kept the overall literary quality respectable," though with a few noted exceptions. Yet Updike eventually turns to what for him is a "crucial question": "What keeps science fiction a minor genre, for all the brilliance of its authors and apparent pertinence of its concerns?"[9]

As American SF writer John Kessel argued in an October 1999 address in Portsmouth, Ohio, titled "Hyperbolic Slang, Maudlin Sentimentalism, and Tragicomic Bubble and Squeak: Science Fiction and the Critics," the question assumes its own conclusion, that science fiction by its very nature is a minor genre. According to Kessel, if science fiction is considered a minor genre, what keeps it in this position is critics like Updike, who bring to science fiction a specific set of criteria for judging literary works that fail to account for or appreciate what science fiction does differently. What SF tends to do differently is to focus less on characterization than on idea—a cardinal sin in the dominant literary aesthetic in English-language fiction since the late 1800s. Or as Farah Mendlesohn puts it, the "reversal of romance, the insistence that romance is *out there* rather than internal, . . . frequently results in non-sf critics judging sf deficient in characterization and emotion."[10]

The assumptions Updike brings to bear upon fiction in general and science fiction in particular are characteristic of the assumptions many literary critics and professors employ when dismissing science fiction as somehow subliterary, although Updike is to be credited with actually reading some of the SF he critiques, unlike most literary critics who dismiss science fiction, who likely do so based on either very little exposure to the genre or complete ignorance of it. Nonetheless, the literary outlook he brings to his reading experience prevents him from fully realizing how science fiction might differ from mainstream realistic fiction and still qualify as literary. In general, such critics' idea of what literature is excludes most science fiction, even if many of them do not know what most science fiction is like.

In contrast, the editors of most college literature anthologies, while exercising a necessary selectivity, do not seem to have limited themselves to such a strict definition of literature, since recent editions of anthologies for survey courses have included a variety of other texts, such as letters or historical documents, in addition to the standard selections of fiction, poetry, drama, and essays. Such readings may be useful to give students some sense of historical and cultural backgrounds in addition to the standard introductory essays, but why dozens of precious pages of such matter when the books' scant space could be given over to presenting an even broader picture of literature?

These decisions are especially puzzling since these literary anthologies are hardly loath to include new writers or selections from previously unanthologized writers in the new editions published predictably every three years or so. One could base a fascinating study of the evolving nature of literary canons, in fact, just by comparing the tables of contents of successive volumes of the same anthology. Almost all freshman readers and survey anthologies published in the last few decades have attempted to expand the canon by including previously neglected or underrepresented writers or groups of writers such as women or minorities. The editors of such books apparently agree with Joanna Russ regarding this expansion of the canon:

> All minority/oppressed art has a wonderful freshness about it (when it is honest) and one of the most heartening things about the last forty-odd years in the United States is the emergence of so many artists who find their grounding in lesbian experience, gay experience, female experience, the experience of being a woman or man of color, being disabled, any combination of the above, and many more.[11]

To be sure, the inclusion of more women writers and writers from various minority groups, besides making readings more relevant for many students, has added fresh voices and talents to our literary experiences. This is entirely consistent with T. S. Eliot's famous statement, in his essay "Tradition and the Individual Talent" (1919), that the canon constantly evolves both in scope and in nature as new writers are added to it.

Accompanying such editorial decisions are introductory essays to many literary anthologies more or less praising themselves for their open-minded inclusiveness, in contrast to older notions of the canon. By way of introduction, for instance, *The Longman Anthology of British Literature* (1999) begins with the remark that "lovers of canonical texts have found themselves sharing the stage with multiculturalists who typically focus on ethnic and minority literatures, usually contemporary and often popular in nature, rather than on earlier and more elite literary productions." Similar rhetoric can be found in other anthologies. The preface to the ninth edition of McGraw-Hill's *American Tradition in Literature* (1999), for example, claims that its volumes are "designed to accommodate the full range and diversity of the American literary tradition." Noting that "any coherent and accurate account of our cultural heritage" entails "knowing a far wider range of authors" than present in earlier anthologies, the preface to the first edition of *The Heath Anthology of American Literature* (1990) seeks to include a greater number of women and minority writers. The third edition of *The Harper Single Volume American Literature* (1999), so says its preface, "reaffirms and invigorates its editors' commitment to provide students with the most comprehensive and reliable introduction to the diversity and depth of American literature."[12]

So just how diverse are such literary anthologies? In terms of periods, gender, ethnicity, and other minorities, and genres such as fiction, poetry, drama, and nonfiction prose, they do rather well. In terms of genres such as science fiction, fantasy, crime fiction, westerns, and so forth, it is as though they do not exist. While the efforts of literary anthologies to include a wide spectrum of writers are admirable, the question arises, if the canon is expanding, where is the science fiction?

Not in most anthologies intended for survey courses in British or American literature, certainly. In American anthologies, one can easily find the fantastic—if not SF—tales of classic authors such as Washington Irving, Nathaniel Hawthorne, and Edgar Allan Poe. But do these anthologies deliver, as *The Norton Anthology of American Literature* promises, "the full range of American literature"? Not if you consider the full range of American literature to include science fiction.

The American volumes of the Norton do just a little better than most of their peers, as they include not only such works as "The Birthmark" (1843) by Hawthorne but also Joanna Russ's "When It Changed" (1972) and Le Guin's "Schrödinger's Cat" (1974). *The Norton Anthology of African American Literature* (1997) includes selections from Samuel R. Delany and Octavia E. Butler, as well as occasional SF author Walter Mosley in his crime-fiction mode. As for some of the others, neither the seventh edition of Prentice Hall's *Anthology of American Literature* (2000) nor *The Heath Anthology of American Literature* includes science fiction, unless one counts Thomas Pynchon's story "Entropy" (1960).

So why would the editors of such anthologies, given their good intentions to offer students "the full range of American literature," give such short shrift to science fiction? A few possibilities come to mind, most immediately ignorance and antipathy. It could be that many anthology editors are simply unaware of much genre fiction, either from lack of interest or because they never had to read it in their own classes or were encouraged to read it outside of class. Or it could be that they are aware that science fiction exists and that some of it might be worth anthologizing, but they are daunted by the sheer bulk of material and have no idea where to start, so they leave it untouched. Its exclusion from their anthologies could also be the result of antipathy, on either their part or the part of their publishers. Some people have tried science fiction and determined that they do not like it; others harbor a hostility toward the genre based on far more limited knowledge.

There are also more complex reasons why science fiction is generally excluded from such anthologies. Some say that students are already familiar with science fiction. Why not instead expose them to things they have not read? Related to this argument is the idea that there is only so much that can be taught; why teach something that many will read on their own anyway?

In any event, the general exclusion of science fiction from anthologies and its limited appearance in the classroom contribute to science fiction's continued marginalization in American literature. This constitutes what might be called a passive reason for its reputation as subliterary or nonliterary. If it is not in literature anthologies or English classes, it must not be worth considering, right?

In addition, one could note that there is what could be called a more active resistance to science fiction. Such attitudes are apparent in Updike's review of the Hartwell anthology and in countless other comments that outsiders have made about the genre beginning with its emergence as a distinct commercial genre in the 1920s. To be sure, much science fiction that has appeared during this time *is* distinctly unliterary, but certainly not all of it is.

The problem, most likely, remains one of categorization and overgeneralization. Limiting ourselves to American fiction, consider the ways in which it is often described or thought about. Employing Sturgeon's Law, one could say that 90 percent of realistic American fiction is crap. But most then do not continue from this assertion and say that *all* mainstream fiction is crap. Suppose, for instance, that on the basis of reading a few novels by Jacqueline Susann and Harold Robbins, one concluded that the American realistic novel was always this unliterary. Yet this seems to be precisely the factor that has led to wholesale condemnations of science fiction: 90 percent of science fiction is crap, therefore, 100 percent of science fiction is crap. This is not only bad math, it is bad criticism. Yet dozens if not hundreds of critics have been guilty of it.

There are also other cultural factors at play. One is a distrust of the popular among many critics and professors. Science fiction is typically considered a branch of popular culture—not surprising, given its pulp-magazine roots and the fact that it has often been published only in paperback (and paperbacks are rarely reviewed, another strike against the genre). Beneath this dismissal of the popular, of course, is an elitism based upon a low estimation of the masses' intelligence and taste, an elitism that could be challenged as more a marker of class sensibilities than aesthetic ones.

But is science fiction really a part of popular culture? If we are talking about science fiction movies or television, with which written science fiction is often but usually erroneously linked in terms of quality, then a connection with popular culture would be warranted. However, though the means of publication are closely allied with mass production and distribution, and though some science fiction writers have reached rather large audiences, by and large written science fiction is not incredibly popular, and many of its authors do not earn enough from their writing to support themselves full time. In fact, some would assert that science fiction, which combines narrative art with often difficult scientific concepts or bizarre imaginative extrapolation, is even less accessible than most forms of writing. As for sales, consider as an example the case of three African

American women writers working in the same eight-year period: at the end of August 2001, Amazon.com ranked Toni Morrison's *Sula* (1974) 2,128th in sales, Octavia E. Butler's *Kindred* (1979) 8,746th, and *The Color Purple* (1982) by Alice Walker 5,920th. Which is more popular, the two "literary" novels about the lives of black women or the science fiction novel about the life of a black woman? And compare these numbers for paperbacks by John Kessel: 80,686th for *Corrupting Dr. Nice* (1998), 292,949th for *Good News from Outer Space* (1995), and 368,268th for *The Pure Product* (1997).

Finally, science fiction's lack of consistently high sales and a shining literary reputation could be attributable to both the factors briefly described here and its own sense of identity and marketing. While many within science fiction dislike the routine dismissal the field often receives, many others are happy not to be associated with the world of what they term "mundane" fiction. Similarly, those who do read science fiction generally prefer to have it clearly marked and separately shelved in bookstores and libraries. These factors too have no doubt contributed to the existing literary reputation of science fiction in the United States.

But this is too easy, too unthinking, like the statements of racists that whites prefer to associate with whites and blacks with blacks. Moreover, the facile dismissal of a whole body of work as unworthy of literary consideration is not only inaccurate but also unfortunate, as it robs readers of the pleasure they might derive from writers unknown to them. To return to Kessel's talk about science fiction and the critics, the title of that talk, "Hyperbolic Slang, Maudlin Sentimentalism, and Tragicomic Bubble and Squeak," comes from a review of a work that was savaged in its own time but has since become an American classic, namely, Herman Melville's *Moby-Dick* (1851). Such are the fortunes of literary reception and reputation, and one hopes that those science fiction writers of our time who deserve greater recognition and respect will ultimately receive it, as Melville did.

Given the relative lack of respect science fiction writers and readers receive in the larger literary world, why do they continue to read and write SF? For the writers there are a variety of reasons, of course. While most SF writers are not best sellers, the typical financial incentives are still enticing, especially since fiction sells better in the United States and elsewhere than other types of writing; additionally, American SF, like American cinema, dominates international markets, and even midlist American SF writers routinely are translated and marketed overseas. Along with sales comes attention, and if most American SF writers are denied the kind of attention granted successful mainstream writers, both popular and literary, they often receive something close to adulation at the many fan conventions and even academic conferences devoted to fantastic literature to which they are routinely invited.[13] Their work is also discussed not only in the SF news magazine *Locus,* fanzines, and, more recently, Internet discussion groups but also in academic journals such as *Extrapolation, Science Fiction Studies, Foundation,* and the *Journal of the Fantastic in the Arts.* Consequently, American SF authors tend to have a greater amount of contact with their readers and with scholars who write about their work than most other authors, and most of this contact is positive.

But the most obvious reason SF authors do what they do and readers continue to read them concerns what is unique to science fiction. For most SF writers, what they want to write simply forms itself into science fiction narratives, as in the case of *The Sparrow* by Mary Doria Russell. Often this impulse originates in the question *what if*? One of the best statements regarding the rationale behind the writing of science fiction is found in Ursula K. Le Guin's 1975 essay "Science Fiction and Mrs. Brown":

> They write science fiction, I imagine, because what they have to say is best said using the tools of science fiction, and the craftsman knows his tools. And still, they are novelists, because while using the great range of imagery available to science fiction, they say what it is they have to say through a character—not a mouthpiece, but a fully realized creation. The character is primary. And what used to be the entire object of science fiction—the invention of miraculous gadgets, the relation of alternate histories, and so on—is now used subjectively, as a metaphor. . . . The writers' interest is no longer really in the gadget, or the size of the universe, or the laws of robotics, or the destiny of social classes, or anything describable in quantitative, or mechanical, or objective terms. They are not interested in what things do, but in how things are. Their subject is the subject, that which cannot be other than subject: ourselves. Human beings.
>
> But these are human beings who live in the universe as seen by modern science, and in the world as transformed by modern technology. That is where science fiction still remains distinct from the rest of fiction.[14]

Similar reasons are voiced by numerous SF writers, critics, and readers. "Unlike any other category of contemporary literature," writes John Clute, "SF is a mode of looking at the world and its potential. Science fiction offers writers an intensely bracing angle of view, especially in a time of constant innovation and crisis."[15] Like Clute emphasizing SF's role as a literature of change but also emphasizing SF as a literature of escapism, Gary K. Wolfe, in a review of *The Collected Stories of Greg Bear* (2003), writes, "People have not always been what they are now, and what they are now will not last. The future is a different country, and it may be strange or dark or unpleasant by our standards, but in SF at least, it's ours for the inventing."[16] Charles N. Brown, a longtime fan and the founder of *Locus*, quotes SF editor Donald A. Wollheim as saying, "SF is literature for adolescents of all ages" and adds, "Adolescents question the world, and SF is the only literature that does that."[17] Besides which, many SF authors claim that science fiction is a pleasure to read, and certainly its readers take pleasure in it.

All told, then, American science fiction since the 1970s has performed a number of functions that account for its creation and its readership. It imaginatively presents readers with unusual but still largely plausible ideas brought to life through stories that are for the most part traditionally plotted and characters who range from the two-dimensional to the fully realized, told in prose that may be experimental in style or structure but that usually is highly readable. It may be comic, satirizing contemporary society, or serious, pointing out the possible consequences of current trends. It takes science and technology seriously, showing how they contribute to the changes that science fiction assumes are inevitable. Contemporary American science fiction across the board is both serious speculation and escape, inquiry and entertainment. At its best, especially the best work of its maturity, it deserves the title "literature" in even its most restrictive sense as well as a greater degree of respect and attention than it currently receives.

Notes

Chapter 1—Introduction

1. Melia, "John Brunner," 19.

2. Wollheim, *Universe Makers,* 16.

3. The February 1997 issue of the *Magazine of Fantasy and Science Fiction* (hereafter *F&SF*) introduced an irregular column by Mike Resnick called "Forgotten Treasures" in response to what Resnick, *F&SF,* and others in the field perceived as an alarming lack of knowledge about older science fiction works among self-proclaimed science fiction fans.

4. Donald M. Hassler, review of *Cosmic Engineers: A Study of Hard Science Fiction,* by Gary Westfahl (Westport, Conn.: Greenwood, 1996), *Extrapolation* 37 (1996): 365.

5. See Franklin's anthology *Future Perfect,* rev. ed., for a selection of such works.

6. For a good survey of works some scholars regard as precursors to science fiction or early science fiction, see the first two volumes of *The Road to Science Fiction,* edited by Gunn.

7. Through this book I shall use SF as an abbreviation for "science fiction." Most writers and critics avoid the popular term "sci fi" as the mark of fans or outsiders.

8. Norman Spinrad, *Child of Fortune* (Toronto: Bantam, 1985), 432.

9. Hellekson, *Alternate History,* 3.

10. Aldiss and Wingrove, *Trillion Year Spree,* 163, where Aldiss contrasts "Burroughsian" science fiction with what he calls the "Wellesian" variety, which is "analytic" as opposed to "fantastic."

11. This is not to say that many of them are not worth reading. Those interested should see Asimov, *Before the Golden Age.*

12. See Knight, *In Search of Wonder;* Atheling, *Issue at Hand* and *More Issues at Hand;* and Amis, *New Maps of Hell.*

13. Heinlein, "On the Writing of Speculative Fiction," 17.

14. Though she was not the first person to use the term, Judith Merril, the closest thing SF in English has had to a Gertrude Stein, popularized it in such publications as her anthology *England Swings SF* (1968).

15. See a brief discussion of this in Harris-Fain, "Farewell to the Master."

16. Westfahl, "Sturgeon's Fallacy," 258. However, Westfahl's claim ultimately hinges upon the fact that in 1993, according to the *MLA International Bibliography,* SF received more scholarly attention than mystery and detective fiction, which he admits is not a strong support for his argument.

Chapter 2—After the New Wave, 1970–1976

1. See Franklin, "Vietnam War as American Science Fiction and Fantasy," for a full discussion of these ads along with SF related to the Vietnam War.

2. In 1970 Asimov's Foundation series included only three books. In response to his growing successes, he began adding more titles to the series in the 1980s.

3. Blish is widely admired as one of the most important writers and critics in American SF of the 1950s and 1960s; ironically, he received the most money and fan mail for his *Star Trek* adaptations and this novel, according to Ketterer.

4. Larry Niven, *Ringworld* (New York: Ballantine, 1970), 300.

5. In 1995 Finney published a sequel to *Time and Again* called *From Time to Time*. Featuring the same protagonist, this novel is set a few decades later, in the early 1900s.

6. See, for instance, Brian Stableford in *Survey of Science Fiction Literature,* who nonetheless concedes that "a good deal of work evidently went into the planning of its background."

7. Robert Silverberg, *A Time of Changes* (Garden City, N.Y.: Doubleday, 1971), 83.

8. Ibid., 85–86.

9. Chapman, *Road to Castle Mount,* 4.

10. Ibid., 8, 64–66.

11. A detailed history of Farmer's progress toward the concepts embodied in the Riverworld series is available in Chapman's *Magic Labyrinth of Philip José Farmer,* 69.

12. Philip José Farmer, *To Your Scattered Bodies Go* (New York: Putnam, 1971), 17–18.

13. Philip José Farmer, *The Fabulous Riverboat* (New York: Putnam, 1971), 74–75.

14. Chapman, *Magic Labyrinth of Philip José Farmer,* 69.

15. See Harris-Fain, "Authentic History, Alternate History, and Alternate Future History" for a general discussion of reading dated futuristic fiction as alternate history or alternate future history.

16. Isaac Asimov, *The Gods Themselves* (Garden City, N.Y.: Doubleday, 1971), 58.

17. Ibid., 53.

18. Patrouch, *Science Fiction of Isaac Asimov,* 267.

19. Hassler, *Isaac Asimov,* 92.

20. For a fuller discussion of the novel, see Clareson, *Understanding Contemporary American Science Fiction,* 259–61, and Cummins, *Understanding Ursula K. Le Guin,* 71–87 and throughout.

21. The connection with the Hebrew woman who brutally slays the Canaanite commander Sisera in the book of Judges is another example of the allusiveness frequently found in New Wave SF. Similarly, the potential self-reflexivity demonstrated by the presence of a contemporary character who shares the same first name as the author shows another postmodern trait found in some of the New Wave.

22. See, for example, Barr's *Future Females* and *Feminist Fabulation;* Bartkowski, *Feminist Utopias;* Lefanu, *In the Chinks of the World Machine;* and Roberts, *New Species.* Also see Sargent, *Women of Wonder,* for a good sampling of SF by women from

the 1940s to the 1990s, as well as lucid introductions by Sargent and lists for further reading.

23. In *The Furies* (1994), Charnas returns to this post-holocaust world, though the novel is set later.

24. Boulter, "Alice James Raccoona Tiptree Sheldon Jr," 5–31; quote from p. 5.

25. Peter Nicholls, "Horror in SF," in *The Encyclopedia of Science Fiction,* ed. Clute and Nicholls, 587.

26. Joe Haldeman, *The Forever War* (New York: St. Martin's Press, 1974), 113.

27. Ibid., 163–64.

28. Republished in 1996 as *Trouble on Triton* (Middletown, Conn.: Wesleyan University Press).

Chapter 3—From Science Fantasy to Hard Science Fiction, 1977–1983

1. Aldiss and Wingrove, *Trillion Year Spree,* 273–74.

2. Many believe Pohl's finest novel was *The Space Merchants* (1953), written in collaboration with C. M. Kornbluth.

3. See, for example, Sven Birkerts's review of Margaret Atwood's *Oryx and Crake* (2003) in the May 18, 2003, *New York Times Book Review,* where he says, "I am going to stick my neck out and just say it: science fiction will never be Literature with a capital 'L,' and this is because it inevitably proceeds from premise rather than character. It sacrifices moral and psychological nuance in favor of more conceptual matters, and elevates scenario over sensibility." Only someone missing the point of contemporary science fiction could say such a thing.

4. The story continues, and more about the alien Heechee is revealed, in *Beyond the Blue Event Horizon* (1980), *Heechee Rendezvous* (1984), *The Annals of the Heechee* (1987), *The Gateway Trip* (1990), and *The Boy Who Would Live Forever* (2004).

5. Aldiss and Wingrove, *Trillion Year Spree,* 361.

6. When this novel is taught in a course on American cultural history, college students report that they never understood the horrors of American slavery until they read this book.

7. Gregory Benford, *Timescape* (New York: Simon and Schuster, 1980), acknowledgments.

8. David Brin, *Sundiver* (New York: Bantam, 1980), 7, 95, 116.

9. David Brin, *Startide Rising* (West Bloomfield, Mich.: Phantasia Press, 1985).

10. Brin, *Sundiver,* 135.

11. Ibid., 216.

12. Aldiss and Wingrove, *Trillion Year Spree,* 418.

13. Brin, *Startide Rising,* 125.

14. Russell Hoban, *Riddley Walker,* expanded ed. (Bloomington: Indiana University Press, 1998), 2.

15. Clute, "Of This World," 120.

16. Though they do not appear in *The Book of the New Sun,* Wolfe's separately published *The Boy Who Hooked the Sun* (1985) and *Empires of Foliage and Flower* (1987) are two of these fables. Additionally, Wolfe's *Castle of the Otter* (1982) is a collection of stories and essays that relate to the novel.

17. Review of *The Citadel of the Autarch, Washington Post Book World,* January 1983, republished in Clute, *Strokes,* 149.

18. John Clute, "Science Fiction from 1980 to the Present," in *Cambridge Companion to Science Fiction,* ed. James and Mendlesohn, 69–70.

19. Clute, *Strokes,* 152.

20. John Clute, "Wolfe, Gene (Rodman)," in *Encyclopedia of Science Fiction,* ed. Clute and Nicholls, 1338.

21. Following Ridley Scott's loose cinematic adaptation of Dick's novel as *Blade Runner* (1982), the book was rereleased with this title.

22. "The Gernsback Continuum" originally appeared in *Universe 11,* ed. Terry Carr, 81–90 (Garden City, N.Y.: Doubleday, 1981) and has been reprinted in a number of collections, including Gibson's own *Burning Chrome* (New York: Arbor House, 1986). In-text page citations refer to the version in *Burning Chrome.*

23. Ivison, *Canadian Fantasy and Science-Fiction Writers.*

24. Octavia E. Butler, "Speech Sounds," in *Bloodchild and Other Stories* (New York: Four Walls Eight Windows, 1995), 95–96.

25. Hartwell, *Age of Wonders,* 190–91.

26. Ibid., 182.

Chapter 4—Cyberpunk and Other Trends, 1984–1992

1. Robert Sheckley to author, e-mail, February 2004.

2. William Gibson, *Neuromancer* (New York: Ace Science Fiction Books, 1984), 3.

3. Ibid., 51; ellipses in original.

4. Credit here belongs to SF writer Bruce Bethke, who coined the term in 1983.

5. Clute, "Science Fiction from 1980 to the Present," 72.

6. John Clute, "Willis, Connie," in *Encyclopedia of Science Fiction,* ed. Clute and Nicholls, 1331.

7. Kurt Vonnegut, *God Bless You, Mr. Rosewater; or, Pearls before Swine* (New York: Holt, Rinehart and Winston, 1965), 27.

8. Ibid., 27–28.

9. Ironically, however, James never took issue with Wells's writing of what was then labeled "scientific romance," even suggesting prior to Wells's *War of the Worlds* (1898) that the two of them collaborate on a novel about Mars—thus showing that the rejection of science fiction in the "literary" world is a twentieth-century phenomenon.

10. Readers who pick up a copy of *Venus on the Half-Shell* (1975), a science fiction novel ascribed to author Kilgore Trout,

might assume it was written pseudonymously by Vonnegut, but in fact it is the work of SF writer Philip José Farmer.

11. A thorough analysis of this book and of Le Guin's technique can be found in Cummins, *Understanding Ursula K. Le Guin,* 176–96.

12. This story, written by Kessel, has also been published separately as "Faustfeathers."

13. Specifically, Pohl made these comments at the 2003 Science Fiction Research Association conference in Guelph, Ontario, and at the 2004 conference in Skokie, Illinois.

14. Further volumes in the series include *Xenocide* (1991), *Children of the Mind* (1996), *Ender's Shadow* (1999), *Shadow of the Hegemon* (2001), *Shadow Puppets* (2002), *First Meetings in the Enderverse* (2003), and *The Shadow Saga 4* (2003).

15. Readers interested in learning more about young-adult science fiction should consult Francis J. Molson and Susan G. Miles's "Young Adult Science Fiction," in *Anatomy of Wonder,* 4th ed., ed. Barron, 393–452; Reid, *Presenting Young Adult Science Fiction;* and Sullivan, *Young Adult Science Fiction.*

16. John Kessel, "Invaders," in his *The Pure Product* (New York: Tor, 1997), 73. In-text citations are to this version.

17. John Kessel, "Buffalo," in *Meeting in Infinity* (Sauk City, Wis.: Arkham House, 1992), 282.

18. Hall, "Charles N. Brown," 92.

19. Hassler, "*Dhalgren,*" 335.

Chapter 5—Anything Goes, 1993–2000

1. Edward James, "The Landscape of Mars," *Times Literary Supplement,* May 3, 1996, 23.

2. The term "terraforming," coined by SF writer Jack Williamson decades earlier, refers to the concept of converting the ecosystem of other planets or moons to make them like Earth.

3. Russell Letson, "*Locus* Looks at Books," *Locus* 31 (November 1993): 19.

4. Clute, *Look at the Evidence*, 386.

5. First published in 1912 as "Under the Moons of Mars" under the pseudonym Norman Bean in the pulp publication *All-Story Magazine*.

6. The phrase "shorter series" is relative here. For instance, Cherryh's Chanur series includes five books.

7. The other volumes in the trilogy are *Beggars and Choosers* (1994) and *Beggars Ride* (1996).

8. Although the observations here are my own, I am indebted to Franko for her comparisons between Kress's Beggars trilogy and Rand's *Atlas Shrugged*.

9. Thomas D. Clareson, interview with author, Wooster, Ohio, winter 1993.

10. See Weil and Wolfe, *Harlan Ellison*, 243–47.

11. At the same time, several British SF writers have suffered in terms of reputation because of their association with SF, and even Banks, who has accomplished the rare feat of achieving acclaim as both a realistic novelist and a science fiction writer, distinguishes the latter by the use of his middle initial in his byline.

12. Ironically, Haldeman jokingly claims that had the novella he submitted to Harlan Ellison in the 1970s, titled *Fantasy for Six Electrodes and One Adrenaline Drip*, appeared in the projected but never-published "The Last Dangerous Visions," he would have "invented" cyberpunk a decade before it first appeared.

13. While Chiang's treatment of this concept is original, the concept itself is not. The alien Tralfamadorians in Kurt Vonnegut Jr.'s *Slaughterhouse-Five* (1969) also experience time simultaneously, as does the transformed Dr. Manhattan in Alan Moore and Dave Gibbons's graphic novel *Watchmen* (1987).

14. Clute, "Science Fiction from 1980 to the Present," 78.

15. Wolfe, "Malebolge," 418.

16. Ibid.

17. Ibid., 417.

18. Wolfe, "Evaporating Genre."

19. Ibid., 27–28.

20. Stableford, "Final Chapter," 55.

21. Wolfe, "Evaporating Genre," 28.

22. Gardner Dozois, "Summation: 2000," in *The Year's Best Science Fiction: Eighteenth Annual Collection,* ed. Gardner Dozois (New York: St. Martin's Press, 2001), xii.

Chapter 6—Conclusion

1. For further discussion, see Westfahl and Slusser, *Science Fiction;* Easterbrook, "Hybrids between Mundane and Maligned"; and Barr, "Textism."

2. Gary K. Wolfe, "Genius Loci," *Locus* 49 (September 2002): 40.

3. Wolfe, "Malebolge," 411.

4. John Updike, "Awriiiighhhhhhhht!," republished in his *More Matter: Essays and Criticism* (New York: Knopf, 1999).

5. Specifically, Bloom included Kurt Vonnegut Jr.'s *Cat's Cradle* (1963); Le Guin's *Left Hand of Darkness* (1969); Thomas M. Disch's *On Wings of Song* (1979); and Crowley's *Little, Big* (1981), *Ægypt* (1987), and *Love and Sleep* (1994). See Harold Bloom, *The Western Canon: The Books and School of the Ages* (New York: Harcourt Brace, 1994).

6. These include *Classic Science Fiction Writers* (1994); separate volumes on Vonnegut (2000), *Slaughterhouse-Five* (2001), and *Cat's Cradle* (2002); separate volumes on Ray Bradbury and *Fahrenheit 451* (2001); separate volumes on Le Guin (1986) and *The Left Hand of Darkness* (1987); and, going further back, *Science Fiction Writers of the Golden Age* (1995).

7. Elaine Showalter, "The Risks of Good Teaching: How 1 Professor and 9 T.A.'s Plunged into Pedagogy," *Chronicle of Higher Education,* July 9, 1999, B6.

8. Updike, "Awriiiighhhhhhhht!"

9. Updike, "The Flaming Chalice," reprinted in his *Odd Jobs: Essays and Criticism* (New York: Knopf, 1991).

10. Farah Mendlesohn, "Introduction: Reading Science Fiction," in *Cambridge Companion to Science Fiction*, ed. James and Mendlesohn, 9.

11. Joanna Russ, "*A Boy and His Dog:* The Final Solution," in *To Write Like a Woman*, by Russ, 65.

12. Quotations taken from David Damrosch, ed., *The Longman Anthology of British Literature* (New York: Longman, 1999), 1:xxxiii; George Perkins and Barbara Perkins, eds., *The American Tradition in Literature* (Boston: McGraw-Hill, 1999), xxvii; Paul Lauter, ed., *The Heath Anthology of American Literature* (Lexington, Mass.: D. C. Heath, 1990), xxxv; and Donald McQuade, ed., *The Harper Single Volume American Literature* (New York: Longman, 1999), xxxvii.

13. The major academic conferences where SF writers regularly appear as guests are organized by two groups, the Science Fiction Research Association and the International Association for the Fantastic in the Arts.

14. Ursula K. Le Guin, "Science Fiction and Mrs. Brown," in *Language of the Night,* ed. Susan Wood, 105–6.

15. Clute, "Of This World," 120.

16. Gary K. Wolfe, "*Locus* Looks at Books," *Locus* 49 (October 2002): 19.

17. Hall, "Charles N. Brown," 90.

Bibliography

Also consult the runs of the following journals and periodicals: *Extrapolation; Foundation: The International Review of Science Fiction; Locus: The Newspaper of the Science Fiction Field; New York Review of Science Fiction;* and *Science Fiction Studies.*

Aldiss, Brian W., and David Wingrove. *Trillion Year Spree: The History of Science Fiction.* New York: Atheneum, 1986.

Amis, Kingsley. *New Maps of Hell: A Survey of Science Fiction.* New York: Harcourt, Brace, 1960.

Armitt, Lucie, ed. *Where No Man Has Gone Before: Women and Science Fiction.* London: Routledge, 1991.

Ashley, Mike, and Marshall B. Tymn. *Science Fiction, Fantasy, and Weird Fiction Magazines.* Westport, Conn.: Greenwood, 1985.

Asimov, Isaac, ed. *Before the Golden Age.* 3 vols. Garden City, N.Y.: Doubleday, 1974.

Atheling, William, Jr. [James Blish]. *The Issue at Hand: Studies in Contemporary Magazine Science Fiction.* Chicago: Advent, 1964.

———. *More Issues at Hand: Critical Studies in Contemporary Science Fiction.* Chicago: Advent, 1970.

Attebery, Brian. *Decoding Gender in Science Fiction.* London: Routledge, 2002.

Bainbridge, William S. *Dimensions of Science Fiction.* Cambridge: Harvard University Press, 1986.

Barr, Marleen. *Feminist Fabulation: Space/Postmodern Fiction.* Iowa City: University of Iowa Press, 1992.

———, ed. *Future Females: A Critical Anthology.* Bowling Green, Ohio: Bowling Green State University Popular Press, 1981.

———, ed. *Future Females, the Next Generation: New Voices and Velocities in Feminist Science Fiction Criticism.* Boulder, Colo.: Rowman & Littlefield, 2000.

———. *Lost in Space: Probing Feminist Science Fiction and Beyond.* Chapel Hill: University of North Carolina Press, 1993.

————. "Textism—an Emancipation Proclamation." *PMLA* 119 (2004): 429–41.

Barron, Neil, ed. *Anatomy of Wonder: A Critical Guide to Science Fiction.* 4th ed. New Providence, N.J.: Bowker, 1995; 5th ed. Westport, Conn.: Libraries Unlimited, 2004.

Bartkowski, Frances. *Feminist Utopias.* Lincoln: University of Nebraska Press, 1989.

Bleiler, Richard, ed. *Science Fiction Writers: Critical Studies of the Major Authors from the Early Nineteenth Century to the Present Day.* 2nd ed. New York: Scribner's, 1999.

Boulter, Amanda. "Alice James Raccoona Tiptree Sheldon Jr: Textual Personas in the Short Fiction of Alice Sheldon." *Foundation* 63 (Spring 1995): 5–31.

Bretnor, Reginald, ed. *Modern Science Fiction: Its Meaning and Its Future.* 2nd ed. Chicago: Advent, 1979.

————, ed. *Science Fiction, Today and Tomorrow.* New York: Harper & Row, 1974.

Broderick, Damien. *Reading by Starlight: Postmodern Science Fiction.* London: Routledge, 1995.

Bukatman, Scott. *Terminal Identity: The Virtual Subject in Postmodern Science Fiction.* Durham, N.C.: Duke University Press, 1993.

Chapman, Edgar L. *The Magic Labyrinth of Philip José Farmer.* San Bernardino, Calif.: Borgo, 1984.

————. *The Road to Castle Mount: The Science Fiction of Robert Silverberg.* Westport, Conn.: Greenwood, 1999.

Clareson, Thomas D. *Understanding Contemporary American Science Fiction: The Formative Period (1926–1970).* Columbia: University of South Carolina Press, 1990.

Clute, John. *Look at the Evidence: Essays and Reviews.* Liverpool: Liverpool University Press, 1996.

————. "Of This World: Why Science Fiction Can't Be Dismissed." In *The Salon.com Reader's Guide to Contemporary Authors,* edited by Laura Miller with Adam Begley, 118–21. New York: Penguin, 2000.

——. *Strokes: Essays and Reviews, 1966–1986*. Seattle: Serconia, 1988.

Clute, John, and Peter Nicholls, eds. *The Encyclopedia of Science Fiction*. New York: St. Martin's Press, 1993.

Cowart, David, and Thomas L. Wymer, eds. *Twentieth-Century American Science-Fiction Writers*. 2 vols. Dictionary of Literary Biography 8. Detroit: Gale, 1981.

Cox, F. Brett, ed. *American Fantasy and Science Fiction Writers*. 4 vols. Dictionary of Literary Biography. Detroit: Gale, forthcoming.

Cummins, Elizabeth. *Understanding Ursula K. Le Guin*. Rev. ed. Columbia: University of South Carolina Press, 1993.

del Rey, Lester. *The World of Science Fiction, 1927–1976: The History of a Subculture*. New York: Ballantine, 1979.

Disch, Thomas M. *The Dreams Our Stuff Is Made Of: How Science Fiction Conquered the World*. New York: Free Press, 1998.

Donawerth, Jane L. *Frankenstein's Daughters: Women Writing Science Fiction*. Syracuse, N.Y.: Syracuse University Press, 1997.

Easterbrook, Neil. "Hybrids between Mundane and Maligned." *Science Fiction Studies* 30 (2003): 510–13.

Franklin, H. Bruce, ed. *Future Perfect: American Science Fiction of the Nineteenth Century*. Rev. ed. New Brunswick, N.J.: Rutgers University Press, 1995.

——. "The Vietnam War as American Science Fiction and Fantasy." *Science-Fiction Studies* 17 (1990): 341–59.

Franko, Carol. "What-If-ing the Titans: Nancy Kress's Dialogic Beggars Trilogy." *Extrapolation* 43 (2002): 131–62.

Freedman, Carl. *Critical Theory and Science Fiction*. Hanover, N.H.: University Press of New England / Wesleyan University Press, 2000.

Gunn, James, ed. *The New Encyclopedia of Science Fiction*. New York: Viking, 1988.

——, ed. *The Road to Science Fiction*. Vols. 1 and 2. New York: Mentor, 1977, 1979.

Gunn, James, and Matthew Candelaria, eds. *Speculations on Speculation: Theories of Science Fiction*. Lanham, Md.: Scarecrow, 2004.

Hall, Jennifer A. "Charles N. Brown: The Joy of SF." *Locus* 49 (September 2002): 89f.

Harris-Fain, Darren. "Authentic History, Alternate History, and Alternate Future History in Superhero Graphic Novels, 1986–1996." In *Classic and Iconoclastic Alternate History Science Fiction,* edited by Edgar L. Chapman and Carl Yoke, 141–70. Lewiston, N.Y.: Mellen, 2003.

———. "Farewell to the Master: Standing In for Tom Clareson, Spring 1993." *Science-Fiction Studies* 23 (1996): 423–27.

Hartwell, David. *Age of Wonders: Exploring the World of Science Fiction*. New York: McGraw-Hill, 1984; 2nd ed., New York: Tor, 1996.

Hassler, Donald M. "*Dhalgren, The Beggar's Opera,* and Georgic: Implications for the Nature of Georgic." *Extrapolation* 30 (1989): 332–38.

———. *Isaac Asimov*. Mercer Island, Wash.: Starmont House, 1991.

Hassler, Donald M., and Clyde Wilcox, eds. *Political Science Fiction*. Columbia: University of South Carolina Press, 1997.

Heinlein, Robert A. "On the Writing of Speculative Fiction." In *Of Worlds Beyond: The Science of Science Fiction Writing,* edited by Lloyd Arthur Eshbach, 13–19. Chicago: Advent, 1964.

Hellekson, Karen. *The Alternate History: Refiguring Historical Time*. Kent, Ohio: Kent State University Press, 2001.

Ivison, Douglas, ed. *Canadian Fantasy and Science-Fiction Writers*. Dictionary of Literary Biography 251. Detroit: Gale, 2002.

James, Edward. *Science Fiction in the 20th Century*. Oxford: Oxford University Press/Opus, 1994.

James, Edward, and Farah Mendlesohn, eds. *The Cambridge Companion to Science Fiction*. Cambridge: Cambridge University Press, 2003.

Jones, Gwyneth. *Deconstructing the Starships: Science, Fiction, and Reality.* Liverpool: Liverpool University Press, 1999.

Ketterer, David. *Imprisoned in a Tesseract: The Life and Work of James Blish.* Kent, Ohio: Kent State University Press, 1987.

Knight, Damon. *In Search of Wonder: Essays on Modern Science Fiction.* Rev. ed. Chicago: Advent, 1967.

Landon, Brooks. *Science Fiction after 1900: From the Steam Man to the Stars.* Studies in Literary Themes and Genres 12. New York: Twayne, 1997.

Larbalestier, Justine. *The Battle of the Sexes in Science Fiction.* Middletown, Conn.: Wesleyan University Press, 2002.

Lefanu, Sarah. *In the Chinks of the World Machine: Feminism and Science Fiction.* London: Women's Press, 1988.

Le Guin, Ursula K. *The Language of the Night: Essays on Fantasy and Science Fiction.* Rev. ed. Edited by Susan Wood. New York: HarperCollins, 1992.

Lerner, Frederick Andrew. *Modern Science Fiction and the American Literary Community.* Metuchen, N.J.: Scarecrow, 1985.

Magill, Frank N., ed. *Survey of Science Fiction and Fantasy Literature.* 4 vols. Pasadena, Calif.: Salem, 1996.

———, ed. *Survey of Science Fiction Literature.* 5 vols. Englewood Cliffs, N.J.: Salem, 1979.

Malzberg, Barry N. *The Engines of the Night: Science Fiction in the Eighties.* Garden City, N.Y.: Doubleday, 1982.

Marchesani, Joseph. "Science Fiction and Fantasy." In *The Gay and Lesbian Literary Heritage: A Reader's Companion to the Writers and Their Words, from Antiquity to the Present,* edited by C. J. Summers, 638–44. New York: Holt, 1995.

McCaffery, Larry, ed. *Across the Wounded Galaxies: Interviews with Contemporary American Science Fiction Writers.* Urbana: University of Illinois Press, 1990.

———, ed. *Storming the Reality Studio: A Casebook of Cyberpunk and Postmodern Fiction.* Durham, N.C.: Duke University Press, 1991.

Melia, Sally Ann. "John Brunner." *Interzone* 97 (July 1995): 19f.

Mendlesohn, Farah. "Women in Science Fiction: Six American Sf Writers between 1960 and 1985." *Foundation* 53 (Autumn 1991): 53–69.

Moylan, Tom. *Demand the Impossible: Science Fiction and the Utopian Imagination.* London: Methuen, 1986.

———. *Scraps of the Untainted Sky: Science Fiction, Utopia, Dystopia.* Boulder, Colo.: Westview, 2000.

Patrouch, Joseph F., Jr. *The Science Fiction of Isaac Asimov.* Garden City, N.Y.: Doubleday, 1974.

Pederson, Jay P., ed. *St. James Guide to Science Fiction Writers.* Detroit: St. James, 1996.

Platt, Charles. *Dream Makers: Science Fiction and Fantasy Writers at Work.* New York: Ungar, 1987.

Reid, Susan Elizabeth. *Presenting Young Adult Science Fiction.* New York: Twayne, 1998.

Riemer, James D. "Homosexuality in Science Fiction and Fantasy." In *Erotic Universe: Sexuality and Fantastic Literature,* edited by Donald Palumbo, 145–61. Westport, Conn.: Greenwood, 1986.

Roberts, Robin. *A New Species: Gender and Science in Science Fiction.* Urbana: University of Illinois Press, 1993.

Russ, Joanna. *To Write Like a Woman: Essays in Feminism and Science Fiction.* Bloomington: Indiana University Press, 1995.

Sargent, Pamela, ed. *Women of Wonder.* Rev. ed. 2 vols. San Diego: Harcourt Brace, 1995.

Sayer, Karen, and John Moore, eds. *Science Fiction: Critical Frontiers.* New York: St. Martin's Press, 2000.

Shippey, Tom, ed. *Fictional Space: Essays on Contemporary Science Fiction.* Oxford: Blackwell, 1991.

Slusser, George, and Eric S. Rabkin, eds. *Hard Science Fiction.* Carbondale: Southern Illinois University Press, 1986.

Slusser, George E., and Tom Shippey, eds. *Fiction 2000: Cyberpunk and the Future of Narrative.* Athens: University of Georgia Press, 1992.

Slusser, George, Gary Westfahl, and Eric S. Rabkin, eds. *Science Fiction and Market Realities.* Athens: University of Georgia Press, 1996.

Spinrad, Norman. *Science Fiction in the Real World*. Carbondale: Southern Illinois University Press, 1990.

Stableford, Brian M. "The Final Chapter of the Sociology of Science Fiction." *Foundation* 79 (2000): 41–58.

———. *The Sociology of Science Fiction*. San Bernardino, Calif.: Borgo, 1987.

———. "The Third Generation of Genre Science Fiction." *Science Fiction Studies* 23 (1996): 321–30.

Sullivan, C. W., III, ed. *Young Adult Science Fiction*. Westport, Conn.: Greenwood, 1999.

Weil, Ellen, and Gary K. Wolfe. *Harlan Ellison: The Edge of Forever.* Columbus: Ohio State University Press, 2002.

Westfahl, Gary. *Cosmic Engineers: A Study of Hard Science Fiction*. Westport, Conn.: Greenwood, 1996.

———. "Sturgeon's Fallacy." *Extrapolation* 38 (1997): 255–77.

———. "Where No Market Has Gone Before: 'The Science-Fiction Industry' and the *Star Trek* Industry." *Extrapolation* 37 (1996): 291–301.

Westfahl, Gary, and George Slusser, eds. *Science Fiction, Canonization, Marginalization, and the Academy*. Westport, Conn.: Greenwood, 2002.

Wolfe, Gary K. "Evaporating Genre: Strategies of Dissolution in the Postmodern Fantastic." In *Edging into the Future: Science Fiction and Contemporary Cultural Transformation,* edited by Veronica Hollinger and Joan Gordon, 11–29. Philadelphia: University of Pennsylvania Press, 2002.

———. *The Known and the Unknown: The Iconography of Science Fiction*. Kent, Ohio: Kent State University Press, 1979.

———. "Malebolge, or the Ordnance of Genre." *Conjunctions* 39 (2002): 405–19.

Wollheim, Donald A. *The Universe Makers: Science Fiction Today.* New York: Harper, 1971.

Wolmark, Jenny. *Aliens and Others: Science Fiction, Feminism and Postmodernism*. Iowa City: University of Iowa Press, 1994.

Index